Praise for *200 Essential Preschool Acti*

"*200 Essential Preschool Activities* is a must-have for new and aspiring teachers who want to provide fun, fresh, and highly effective learning activities for young children. Olson provides not only an abundance of activities to choose from but also all the details you need to turn your classroom into a learning playground."

—Barbara Johnson, MA, instructor, Minot State University

"The author is a talented teacher who loves to engage and connect with children in her classroom. This book is written in a way that helps teachers learn to teach through play. The author shows how one fun and enjoyable activity can be used to teach many different skills. You will find that most activities only require what you already have in your classroom. This book is skillfully created and an invaluable guide to working with the young child. As her coworker, I have seen successful academic learning take place—again and again—through these activities."

—Alice Smette, speech pathologist

"Julienne's ideas for creative play are phenomenal. As a physical therapist in many schools, I walk into many kinds of preschool classrooms. The energy in Julienne's room is always calm yet fun. The blend of structure, fun, and learning creates this."

—Erika Hanson, physical therapist,
advanced trainer of the Nurtured Heart Approach

"*200 Essential Preschool Activities* is a well-organized, comprehensive, and functional handbook for parents, educators, child care professionals, and therapists. As an occupational therapist in the school system, I will use Ms. Olson's book as a reference for fine-, gross-, and sensory-motor activity ideas that encourage self-discovery and hands-on learning. This book will become an essential part of your preschool lesson planning!"

—Kristine Morris, occupational therapist

"Julienne Olson has many years of experience in working with preschool children. This book provides an excellent variety of activities to supplement your research-based preschool curriculum."

—Brenda Jordan, director of special education,
Rural Cass County Multidistrict Special Education Unit

"A must-have for all early childhood teachers! *200 Essential Preschool Activities* hits the mark for creating quality, intentional, and developmentally appropriate experiences for young children. Each activity addresses a developmental domain and has a What Are Children Learning? section, which reminds us of the importance of purposeful teaching. In addition, most activities include adaptation and enhancement ideas, which are crucial for addressing the varied learning styles of children. All of the developmental domains are addressed in this book so children's development is supported in these impressionable early years of learning. I especially appreciate the chapter addressing family involvement at home and within the school environment. In these sections, Ms. Olson embraces the home-and-school collaboration as essential to the development of the whole child."

—Kate Keating-Peterson, assistant professor,
Department of Education–Early Childhood, Mayville State University

200 Essential Preschool Activities

200
ESSENTIAL
Preschool Activities

JULIENNE M. OLSON

Redleaf Press®
www.redleafpress.org
800-423-8309

Published by Redleaf Press
10 Yorkton Court
St. Paul, MN 55117
www.redleafpress.org

First edition 2012
Cover design by Jim Handrigan
Cover photograph © Nailia Schwarz/Veer
Interior design by Percolator
Typeset in ITC Slimbach
Printed in the United States of America
19 18 17 16 15 14 13 12   1 2 3 4 5 6 7 8

Library of Congress Cataloging-in-Publication Data
Olson, Julienne M.
   200 essential preschool activities / Julienne M. Olson.
     pages cm
   ISBN 978-1-60554-104-4 (alk. paper)
   1. Education, Preschool—Activity programs.   I. Title. II. Title: Two hundred essential
preschool activities.
   LB1140.35.C74O57 2012
   372.21—dc23
                               2012007939

Printed on acid-free paper

Thank you to all of the student teachers I have worked with over the years. You have kept me creative and have motivated me to search for fresh new ideas. To the families I have worked with: your children are the reason for this book. A special thank you to Deanne Borgeson for encouraging me and helping me find the path to complete this project.

—J.O.

Contents

CHAPTER 5
Learning Games 153

CHAPTER 6
Family Involvement 191

**INVOLVING FAMILIES
IN THE HOME SETTING**

**INVOLVING FAMILIES
IN THE SCHOOL SETTING**

Preface

I stood up one day and looked around my early childhood classroom. The volume was excessively high, and the children were busy dumping out boxes of toys and quickly moving on to the next item. They were not engaged and seemed to be constantly squabbling for attention. One little girl, who seemed to prefer observing the scene rather than tossing herself into the stormy sea, came over to stand beside me. She looked up and declared, "Well, we sure aren't in Kansas anymore."

What was happening was a lack of structure and planning on my part. I quickly realized that I was filling time in the day. My directives to the children went like this:

"Go do puzzles."

"Here is a box of blocks."

"Go look at some picture books."

The children were great, but I needed to change. They deserved lessons that were created to promote learning, functional skills, and interaction. They needed structure, boundaries, and well-thought-out activities.

That was the beginning of this book. The ideas you find here will help children be creative, learn new skills, and build relationships with their peers. Please know that there is a difference between overbearing boundaries and well-planned activities. Structure doesn't need to limit children's experiences.

Some preschoolers need a direction and are then able to take the play to their own level of imagination. Let me tell you a story about a child like that. As this particular boy sat on the couch watching his friends, I sat down and said to him,

"Is this your car? Can you take me to the park?" Pretty soon, he turned the beanbag chair into Santa's sack, placed all the stuffed animals on top as the toys, and recruited four friends to jump around in front of him as reindeer. All I had to do was to give him an idea—and then let the play evolve.

This book was written primarily for student teachers and new teachers in early childhood or early childhood special education. However, it also provides veteran teachers with ideas that will help them refresh their love of teaching and spark their creativity.

Most teachers are proficient in finding activities. Although this book is activity based, it is written to encourage teachers to think about *why* they are using an activity and *how* to use the lesson to enhance learning. The activities are a foundation for lesson planning and include adaptations for many different skill levels. The ideas complement curriculum and can be used with numerous topics and a variety of literature. Each lesson is based on common knowledge of the development of young children and on my years of experience working with preschoolers.

I have been an early childhood special education teacher since 1995. I have never found a yellow-brick path or a magical wizard to make sure I was on track. We do need to allow children to break out of their shells, find their wings, and learn to fly. Wouldn't it be wonderful if we could provide them with enough wind to help them soar over the mountains?

CHAPTER 1

Classroom Structure

Structuring a classroom requires careful thought and planning. Many factors should be considered when you set up different areas of an early childhood room to make smooth transitions throughout the day. Because of the complexities involved, many of the topics in this chapter are broad in scope and involve multiple learning domains. The ideas are not all encompassing; rather, they're intended to provide you with a place to start planning so you can adapt them to fit your own unique setting. What you will find are tips and suggestions on how to make a classroom predictable and consistent for children.

Why is this chapter so important? With a well-thought-out classroom structure designed to promote learning, you can expect to see an increase in independence, comfort, and positive behavior in children. The ideas can quickly be applied to any classroom setting so a new school year can begin with consistency and engaged learning.

ACTIVITY 1

 Plan an Effective Room Design

Every teacher's goal should be to set up the classroom to promote learning for children in a stable environment. Here are some tips to keep your room organized while creating centers that help children stay engaged.

- As you set up different areas in your room, block the areas off with bulletin boards or barriers.
- Hang material over shelves of toys that are not currently being used. This keeps your classroom looking organized.
- When changing centers in your room, change only one thing at a time so children are surrounded by consistency.
- Have children help when you change centers.
- Rotate the toys on the toy shelves frequently. This will help the children stay interested and excited to see what they can play with next.
- Keep some toys to use in centers only. These will remain high-interest items because they are not available during free-play time.
- Develop routines for different areas and transitions in your room to keep the flow of the day structured, so students know what to expect.
- Have a quiet area where children can go to calm down or take a break.
- Have at least one large open space for gross-motor movement, musical games, and exploring toys.
- Add common household items to toys or centers, such as paper rolls with the blocks or cleaned-out food containers in the kitchen area.
- If you don't have a coatroom, place cards with students' names on them around the classroom. Children take all their end-of-day clothing and items to that card so they have their own space in which to get ready. This helps them stay organized and responsible for their own things. It also alleviates the typical crowding around coat hooks.
- Put labels on items and areas in the classroom to promote literacy and language.
- Use wall space to display children's work and also as functional spaces to display items that teach colors, concepts, numbers, and shapes. Think about what you are putting on the walls and how each item will help children learn.
- Label toy containers with photographs of the toys stored there so children know where to put materials when they are done. Do the same for shelves where crayons, scissors, paper, or glue are stored.
- Always think about the reason for setting up or moving items and centers in your classroom. Make sure your reason is related to children's learning. Think about how each area promotes the different learning domains, such as language, cognitive growth, fine-motor skills, gross-motor skills, social-emotional skills, and daily living skills. Your classroom should be inviting and organized, with many areas that enhance children's experiences.

ACTIVITY 2

 Write the First Letter Home

This is a sample letter that you could send to parents before the first day they bring their child to school. Teachers must remember that this is an emotional time for parents. We need to make sure they feel comfortable so we can help their children feel secure from the beginning. This is the best way to help new children feel ready for learning.

Dear [Family],

We are eager to welcome [child] on [date]! Dropping your child at the program can be scary both for parents and children. Here are some tips to help you and your child during the first few days.

Before your child starts, begin talking to your child about where he or she will be going and what a day there might be like. Take note of the times when your child will be dropped off and picked up from the program. Make comments like, "When school starts, this is the time we would be leaving" or "I will be waiting to pick you up from school right now."

Visit us to help make your child comfortable about being away from home. While here, take some pictures of the different centers and toys. Then, display and discuss them at home so your child becomes comfortable and knows what to expect. Also meet the teacher(s), take photos, and practice learning names.

Mark the first day on the calendar and start a back-to-school countdown. Plan a fun activity after the first day, like getting a treat or going to visit someone special in your child's life.

Send along a photo of yourself or a favorite toy on the first day for your child to look at. Having something familiar from home is often a comfort.

You want your child to feel good about being here. Be sure you model your own comfort around your child's new adventure! The suggestions below can help you do that on the first day.

DO

- Give your child a hug.
- Make comments like "I know you are going to have a great day. I will pick you up after school" or "I can't wait to pick you up and hear about all the fun things you did at school." Make sure your child sees and hears that you are comfortable and enthusiastic.
- Wait until you have left the classroom to show emotion. It is hard for some parents to leave their child.

- Call to check on your child if you are worried. I am more than happy to let you know how your child is doing and work with you to help you and your child make a smooth transition.
- Be strong for your child. I have hugged many crying children as their parents leave the room. Typically they cry only a few minutes before seeing the toys and other children and deciding to play.

DON'T

- Come back again and again for hugs. When you do this, you are showing your child that you are unsure about leaving. If you stay for three hugs on day 1, your child will try for four the next time, then five, six, seven . . .
- Sneak out of the classroom. This does not build trust. You are teaching your child that you might disappear at any time; as a result, she or he will cling to you even more. I am happy to comfort your child when you leave and will make sure every

child is safe. Many children will cry or scream the first several times that a parent leaves. I have dealt with this many times, and I am confident that your child will learn how to enjoy coming in, *with our help*. If you confidently tell your child "good-bye" and come back on time after class, your child will learn to rely on that information and trust that you will be there every day after school. Eventually this will help your child let you go at the beginning of the school day.

One of my most important jobs is to help your child become confident and secure. This starts when he or she enters the classroom for the very first time. With your help, we can make this transition a positive experience.

Sincerely yours,

ACTIVITY 3

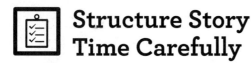 **Structure Story Time Carefully**

Many preschool classrooms cover several topics during story or circle time activities. Working with a calendar, reading a story, playing pre-academic games, doing group fingerplays, learning songs, and practicing personal information are all areas that can be covered during story time. Story or circle time is, at its core, a group lesson, and it should be consistent and predictable.

I like to focus this time on a book. Children love to hear books read over and over. Choose a book instead of a topic as the theme for the week in your classroom. Read that story to the class each day and use ideas from the book as a basis for fine-motor-skill development, center activities, language enhancement, and gross-motor-skill fun throughout the remainder of the day.

HELP CHILDREN UNDERSTAND SEQUENCE

Because story time is a whole-class activity, it needs to be carefully constructed to stay on track. Children attend better to what is happening when they understand the sequence of these events.

USE VISUALS TO SHOW SEQUENCE

Make a small poster and pictures related to your book to represent the different sections you will read during story time. Display these on a bulletin board. For example, when reading a farm book, you might have a poster of a barn and pictures of farm animals that can be placed on the barn after you read each section. Make a pocket for each section of your story time and attach these close to your small poster. For example, have one pocket for reading the book, one for calendar work, one for a fingerplay, and one for a learning game. Put pictures on the pockets to represent each of these areas.

Place one picture that relates to your lessons in each pocket at the beginning of this lesson. Then, for example, when you complete the calendar portion, have a child come up and move the picture from the calendar pocket to the poster. After you read the book, have another child move the story picture to the poster. Continue with this sequence until your story time lesson is finished, all the pockets are empty, and the pictures have been moved to the poster. Make your pictures large enough so they stick out of the pocket and children can see if the pockets are full or empty. This helps children understand what is finished, what is next, and how much longer they will be involved. Keep the number of sections consistent and limited to three or four so the children remain engaged in the story activities. Reinforce children who are paying attention by choosing them to put the pieces on the poster. This often refocuses the rest of the class.

As they move the pieces, ask questions or encourage the children to share their knowledge about the theme. Talk about how many topics they've completed and how many are left, or make up a song to sing between sections.

ALLOW CHILDREN TO MOVE

Story time doesn't have to be a sitting-still activity. Allow children to move. If chairs are used, invite children to sit on the floor when the story is read and return to their chairs for the game and calendar time. Create pre-academic group lessons involving movement that match your book topic. For example, during a farm story, you might encourage children to move around the classroom to find farm animals you have hidden. Talk about where the animals were found. Reinforce position concepts such as *in*, *behind*, *beside*, or *on* every time children bring an animal to the front and place them around the barn. Discuss the role of each animal in the story.

CHOOSE BOOKS CAREFULLY

Find books with good pictures. Make sure that illustrations are not too detailed because children may have trouble focusing on the important themes. Be aware of this when evaluating the text as well. Books that are wordy or have too many new words can be confusing for young children.

It is good to introduce new vocabulary, but make sure you are not featuring too many new words at one time. Books with rhymes or repetitive phrases are good for class participation. Librarians are wonderful resources to help you find good, motivating literature.

READ WITH GUSTO

When reading to children, be expressive and enthusiastic. Make sounds for the fire alarm, quack like the duck, and use a deep voice for the lion or bear. Even though you might feel silly, you will discover how this dramatic presentation holds the attention of your class. Children will remember you for these antics (and I have discovered other teachers waiting outside my door to hear how a story ends).

Whenever possible, memorize the book you are going to read to the children. When you do this, you can pay attention to children's reactions, make eye contact, and help refocus their attention when needed instead of keeping your eyes on the text. Tell the story slowly and clearly, avoid rushing through it.

ADD VARIETY

Figure out different ways to tell the story as you go through the week. Make your own flannel board pieces or find items from the story to bring out as you read. There are also many commercial products that go along with books. Audiocassettes, CDs, DVDs, and MP3 files offer different ways to share the story with your students. Puppets and stuffed animals are always a hit too! Give an animal to one child and have her pass it on every time you turn the page. This helps the children to pay attention to the story.

Share the wonder of literature with children. They will pick up on the joy you feel while you're reading books. This creates a solid foundation for love of reading throughout their own lives.

ACTIVITY 4

Make Snacktime Count!

Snacktime is a prime opportunity to teach children social skills and manners while refining their conversational abilities. In addition, the children can practice passing items, pouring drinks, and making requests. They can also learn the importance of washing their hands before eating or handling food. Talk to them about germs and how they can be transferred from our hands to our food.

TEACH LANGUAGE SKILLS

Children should use language to ask for food items, glasses, straws, and napkins. Help them use complete sentences when making requests. Remind them to use "please" and "thank you." As children become comfortable with snacktime routines, have them take turns distributing food and pouring drinks for their classmates. Pouring drinks is a great fine-motor skill that takes practice to master. While children are serving food, they are also conversing with their friends and learning how to use one-to-one mathematical correspondence to make sure each person gets a snack, cup, or napkin.

INTRODUCE SCIENCE CONCEPTS

Connect snacktime to science: talk about different parts of food, such as the skin and seeds. Have children share their ideas about where foods come from. Where do we get bananas, milk, or carrots? How do foods smell and feel? What colors do the children see? Does the food's color change when they cut it in half to see what is inside?

Other learning possibilities abound during snacktime. Many of the lessons are useful for a lifetime. Children can learn about good eating habits, discriminating between healthy foods and those that should be eaten in moderation. They can learn about food categories, such as dairy, fruits, and vegetables. Help them try new foods at snacktime, knowing that it often takes many trials for them to acquire a taste for certain foods.

Encourage them to have one bite of each new item to decide if it is something they like or dislike. Talk to them about how food tastes and feels in the mouth, using words like *sweet*, *salty*, *sour*, *hot*, and *cold*.

REINFORCE SOCIAL SKILLS

Table manners are another life skill that we can teach. Help children hold silverware and use the side of a fork to cut soft foods. Expect them to use a napkin and to be responsible for their own space at snacktime. They can clear their spot and clean their own hands and face. Be sure to supply a mirror so they can see what they need to wash. Some children may want to wash the tables after snack or push in the chairs.

Often during snacktime the teacher serves the items and stands around the classroom. Instead, sit down with the children and engage them in conversations with you and their peers. Create a mealtime family atmosphere during snack.

You can see the rich potential of snacktime for learning. It should be a well-thought-out part of a preschooler's day, not a break from teaching. Take advantage of it!

ACTIVITY 5

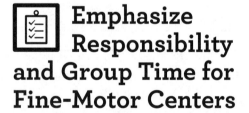

Emphasize Responsibility and Group Time for Fine-Motor Centers

Fine-motor activities are challenging for many children and are often avoided by those who struggle with cutting and coloring skills. Creating daily small groups for fine-motor practice helps children learn how to be a part of a group and to organize their efforts while they receive the practice they need.

PROVIDE SUPPORT

Help children be responsible for gathering and returning the items they need for each activity. Set up a Velcro board with pictures of the different items needed for a fine-motor project. For example, children may need scissors and glue or markers and a pencil. They can look at the board to find the needed items. This Velcro board can be changed quickly each day to include the items required for individual projects. Keep fine-motor supplies in a consistent place or out on a shelf so children don't have to hunt for their supplies. If you want them to have their own items, you should still separate all markers, glue, scissors, and so on into their own containers. Then add children's names to the individual items. This helps them practice finding their written name and categorizing items as they put their supplies away.

Alternatively, if you have a voice recorder, you could record a list of the needed items each time. The children push the switch to hear what supplies they need, memorize the list, and then gather the items. The Velcro board meets the needs of visual learners, while the recording works for auditory learners.

ACTIVITY 6

Make Transitions Smooth

Transitions are an important part of young children's day. Children need to know what is coming next and have the opportunity to prepare themselves and finish up the projects they have been working on. Offer visual and auditory cues for transitions. Make the cues unique to each activity change. For example, use a maraca or tambourine to indicate the time to go to music. Use a red light or lights-out as a cue to clean up after free play.

During transitions, children learn that their teacher is consistent and organized. They learn where things belong and how to match items to containers. They also work together and learn a routine in your classroom.

UTILIZE OPPORTUNITIES FOR LEARNING

With the potential for so much learning, you need to think carefully about each transition.

For example, there are some longer transitions between activities—such as when children are finishing snack. Have something out for the children to remain engaged with. Have a designated area for these longer transitions when you are waiting for the group to come back together so the wait becomes part of your overall day. Use a bell, shaker, or rain stick to cue the end of that time. Surprises are fun, but you don't want children to feel anxious on a regular basis about what is coming next.

USE CLEANUP TIME WISELY

Cleanup is another transitional period worth your consideration. Give children warnings for cleaning up, and be sure to stick to the time frame. If you tell children, "Two minutes until cleanup time," don't become distracted and give them fifteen minutes instead. They need to learn how long two minutes is. Teach them your expectations about that time frame. For example, if you say "Two minutes," that means they can't bring out any new toys. When you say, "One minute left," they need to start finding containers so they can put the toys away. Be a good model for this skill by cleaning up with them. You might teach the children a cleanup song and then sing that when it is time to put away the toys. Help them learn where the items go in your classroom so they can work with you to keep order and organization.

Cleanup is one of the more distinct transitions, so a visual timer with red, yellow, and green lights and sounds for each step is a great three-step visual and auditory tool for children. Alternatively, you can make colored cards to hold up if you don't have an electronic timer. When it is time to clean up, say, "Freeze, hands on your knees!" Then do a countdown from ten. This helps the children stop what they are working on and become focused on the new task of cleaning up. When you get to "one," sing a cleanup song with the class as you put items away in the room. The children move to the next thing from this first transition.

A MODEL ROUTINE

The following is a plan for how transitions can be included in a typical half-day session. You may need more or fewer cues, depending on how you structure the day in your program.

- When children arrive at school, they put their coats and backpacks in a designated area and move on to choose desired toys for free play. At the end of free play, use one of the cleanup techniques mentioned earlier to transition to story time.

- After story time, the children transition to hand washing and snack, which are more natural transitions and don't typically need cues. Instead of having the children go to wash hands all at once, have them leave story time one by one as they share their favorite character from the book or answer a question that you want them to work on. (For example: What is your address? How old are you?) When this strategy is used, the line at the sink isn't too crowded or too long.

- When snack is finished, children pack bags with any mail or papers and then go to a designated transition area in the room. (When you have the children pack in the middle of the day, you alleviate that added chore at the end of the session, when they need to be focused on gathering backpacks and performing dressing skills.)

- Put out different materials each day for the children to explore in the transition area after snack—for example, books, puzzles, drawing materials, pegboards, songs, and blocks. The materials need to involve open-ended play so children can use them for a longer time if they are done early or for just a short time if they only have a few minutes. When the majority of children have arrived in the transition spot, again give them two-minute and then one-minute warnings. When it is time, use a rain stick or other visual and auditory cue to let them know they should move on to your centers or choice board activities. (See activity 7.)

- After your center time, children move to music. Again, you may want to provide a one- and two-minute warning before this transition, using a tambourine or maraca auditory cue. When music time is over, have children react to their day by sharing their favorite lesson or telling which friends they enjoyed playing with before moving to the coat area to get their items before dismissal. When the children are ready and lined up, have a favorite good-bye song or saying to use as they leave the room.

INTRODUCE A LANGUAGE CUE

Teach your students about the word *ready*. What does *ready* look like? What does *ready* sound like? When you say to your students, "Show me that you are ready," they should know that means stopping whatever they are doing and sitting quietly, hands to themselves and eyes on you. This is a great cue for students to learn so you can gain their attention and give directions or redirect behaviors.

Remember, transitions need to be integrated into the day and used as teaching moments. Small transitions help children anticipate what is coming next and feel confident and secure about their day and the consistency of the classroom.

ACTIVITY 7

Create a Choice Board

Here's a way to organize how children move between different centers. Cut a large piece of plywood into a square 3 × 3 feet. Get a piece of felt to cover the board, and sew onto it twenty felt pockets in five rows (four pockets per row). Make tickets that will fit into the pockets with pictures of different areas of the classroom that might be open during center times. Make a corresponding tagboard pocket for each area. Before the children arrive, put tickets into each felt pocket, thinking carefully about the number of children who should be in an area at one time. This will depend on several factors, including how many children are in your classroom, how much supervision is needed in the different areas, and the amount of time you have allotted for centers. (For each cen-

ter described in chapter 2, I suggest the number of children.) At the appropriate time, children take a ticket from the board and match it to the tagboard pocket for the area they have chosen. They put the ticket in the pocket and can then play and interact with the available materials. When they are finished, they take their tickets back and make another choice.

USE A TIMER

Sometimes there is an area that children would stay at for the entire length of your center time. At these centers, you might want to use a timer. Have children take their tickets back when the timer goes off, so other students can have a turn. Other children might go to different areas and stay only seconds and never get involved. These children also might need a timer to encourage them to try an area for a specified length of time before they can make another choice. Each child is unique, and you will need to find what works best for certain students and make changes to your plans as needed.

ORGANIZE TEAMS

You might want all children to try some activities. If you grouped them into teams, you can call a team over during your choice board time for an activity. Make a special colored stick or ticket for them to collect when it is time for their team project. Remember to give them warnings for this transition: "One minute until I need the blue team." Using teams during the choice time ensures that you can spend time with each child and make certain that all of them are learning important skills that they might be reluctant to explore.

ACTIVITY 8

Include Regular Computer Time

As educators, we must keep up with current technology. Can you imagine what today's preschoolers are going to have to know when they leave school? Technology will be a central part of our students' lives, and we need to take every opportunity to help them get a positive start for what is coming. Introduce technology in your classroom and use computers consistently during free play or center time. Give children time to explore computers and learn their different parts, like the screen, monitor, mouse, and keyboard. Show them how to turn on computers and open games.

FOSTER SKILL DEVELOPMENT

There are many computer games that are age appropriate and focus on academic skills. Children can use the keyboard to write their name or find the letters of the alphabet. When children ask about an animal, you can go online and find a picture or information to answer their questions. Have the children beside you when you do the search, and talk them through what you are doing. Have them move the mouse to the correct spot on the screen and click it to activate the website. Know some great websites that offer learning opportunities. Be sure to review these sites—and all computer-based media—in advance to ensure that their content is appropriate for children. Use the computer to take children to new places. If you can't take the children to sled in the snow or visit a zoo, use the computer to watch a video of children sledding or to find a virtual zoo tour.

COMMUNICATE WITH FAMILIES

You might also reach out to families through computer time. If you have the e-mail addresses of children's family members, children can dictate a message to them about their favorite thing to do at school or what they are learning today. Have children choose clip art to add to the e-mail and help them find the letters to type out their own names. Research websites and find good educational materials and games. Send a list of these sites home and encourage families to use computers with their children. Set up a blog as a way to share pictures, information, and events from your classroom. Remember to get written permission from parents before posting photos of children online.

Sing Out Loud

Music is an important part of all preschool classrooms. Thank goodness children don't mind that we sometimes sing off-key! Always sing with enthusiasm and joy during music time.

INVOLVE ALL LEARNING STYLES

Remember that some children are visual learners and that music is an auditory activity. Provide your visual children with visual cues that help them understand musical ideas and concepts. When singing "Twinkle, Twinkle, Little Star," for example, give the children a paper star on a stick to hold up during the song. Finger puppets—such as of spiders or bees—help children participate in favorite fingerplays.

Music helps children learn rhythm. They memorize lyrics and find the beat in the songs. Children feel the beat in their bodies and can be inspired to move to the sounds. They get exercise as they perform actions to the songs and move about the classroom, pretending to be farm animals or jumping beans. Scarves are a fun addition to music. Children can move them quickly or slowly to accompany the tempo.

USE INSTRUMENTS

Musical instruments help children play along with the songs. Bring guests who play different musical instruments into your classroom and ask them to demonstrate to the children how to play. Take your class to a band or choir practice. Hold your own concert with favorite songs, and invite parents or grandparents for a preschool program.

HARNESS THE POWER OF MUSIC

Use music to keep an even tempo in your room. If children are anxious, turn on soft, soothing music. If they have too much energy, stop and do a song with big movements that will help them refocus. Use music to help children with transitions.

Have a song at the beginning of your day and a song that you sing while children are leaving the room. Explore many different types of music and cultural sounds throughout the year. Help children to develop an appreciation for the beauty and harmony of sound.

ACTIVITY 10

 # Say Good-Bye Calmly

Children need routines so they know what is coming and how to prepare. Your routine at the end of the day is just as important as your language group, fine-motor project, or music time. Leave enough time at the end of the day to make this routine comfortable and calm. Don't allow children to leave your room in a rush or filled with anxiety. Have children pack up any mail they have before the end of the day. (As suggested in activity 6, after snack is a good time to pack their bags.)

Help children stay focused by placing a construction paper name card with each child's pic-

ture in different places in the classroom. Try to use the same places each day so children know right away where they need to go. Have them take all items to that spot and get ready there. This eliminates any pileup of clothing and backpacks and gives children their own spaces in which to work. Have them raise their hands if they need assistance. When they are ready, they can line up at a designated spot.

Have a favorite good-bye song to sing each day. The children will remind you to sing it if you forget! Then walk out of the room together in a line, practicing hallway rules as you move through the building toward buses, parents, and after-school rides.

If some of the children are always ready quickly for this routine, you can assign them a partner to help. This allows you to be with another child and helps both children learn how to work together. The helper gets a sense of pride and accomplishment by assisting a friend. This skill often transfers to other parts of the school day, and children learn valuable leadership skills.

CHAPTER 2

Creative Centers

This chapter describes how to create functional centers in an early childhood classroom. It is divided into two sections: Dramatic Play Areas and Discovery and Sensory Areas. Each activity guide presents ideas about structuring the center and encouraging children to work together. These centers are rich with learning opportunities. For example, most centers help children develop conversational language, cooperation, and role-playing skills. In centers, children also learn how to use materials in the classroom and enact scenarios they may encounter in their real-world communities. They also develop academic skills.

For the centers presented in this chapter, a key skill is highlighted at the beginning of each activity guide, but the learning certainly is not limited to this skill. (See the What Are Children Learning? section in each activity guide to get a sense of the richness of the lessons.) Most of these centers should be available in the classroom for one or two weeks and rotated throughout the school year to keep interest levels high.

Centers do require planning and time for collecting materials, setup, and switching. Nonetheless, the social interactions and skill development you will observe in the children make the effort worthwhile. Centers can start out very simply, with just a few items of interest, and materials can be added each year to enhance the play.

ACTIVITY 11
Time to Shop

REAL-WORLD ROLE PLAY

MATERIALS

○ Empty grocery items from home, with pictures of each item

○ Play cash register with pretend money

○ Connecting blocks

○ Plastic or paper grocery bags

○ Large poster board

○ Velcro fasteners

○ Grocery carts or baskets

○ Sample credit cards received in the mail

NUMBER OF CHILDREN AT CENTER

3 to 4

SETUP

● When setting up this grocery store, add posters or advertisements from local grocery stores to decorate the area. Be sure all empty containers are washed clean and free of any food or food stains. The pictures of each item can be symbols, actual photos, or pieces from the containers.

● Make a scanner out of the connecting blocks to go with the cash register.

● Have a shelf for your grocery items and a table where the children can go to check out.

● A long black piece of laminated paper can be wrapped around a small tabletop so the children can slide the groceries on the conveyer belt.

● Make a poster with Velcro strips. This board will hold the pictures of your items. Make laminated handheld sheets that become the grocery lists. Each sheet will have five or six pieces of Velcro on it.

CENTER ACTIONS

The children take turns playing the cashier, customers, and store clerk. The customers should have play money or a credit card. They take a grocery list and choose five to six items from the large poster to stick onto the list. Then they pick a cart or basket and head to the store to find the items on their list. When they have found everything on the list, they place the items on the conveyer belt, and the cashier starts to check them out. The cashier uses the scanner to read the barcode on each item. (Children love making the *beep* as they scan each item.) Then the cashier collects the money or has the customer use a credit card, signing her name on a sticky note. The store clerk bags the purchases and then restocks the shelves after the customer leaves.

WHAT ARE CHILDREN LEARNING?

This activity mimics what happens when children go to the grocery store with a family member. It is also a functional way to role-play: children pretend to be a cashier, scan the barcodes, and bag the items. Children are learning about food labels, money, and job roles. They are practicing matching skills. They can also learn about food groups, such as fruits and vegetables, and about how to choose healthy food instead of junk food.

In the social realm, children are learning how to ask for items from their peers. They are helping each other find the items they want. They often pretend to be father and daughter or husband and wife as they go to the store to shop. They talk about the foods and what items they like to eat.

continued

ADAPTATION AND ENHANCEMENT IDEAS

- Many local stores are willing to donate one or two shopping baskets to add to your center if you don't have child-sized carts. If you do not have a play cash register, you can easily make one out of a box by cutting the top so it can flip up and hold the money.

- Purses or wallets can be added to the center so children can carry money.

- Aprons can be worn by the store workers.

- For some children, you might need to place pictures on the poster that are an exact match to the grocery items. Experiment with the number of items you want in your store. Too many items can be frustrating for children to hunt through. Be aware of your space and what you have room for. Grocery items can change each year so you don't need to store boxes if you don't have the space.

- Be sure to demonstrate how this area works before letting children use it to create their own scenarios. The grocery area is often a place where children get into the cycle of putting all the boxes in a bag and then dumping them out without any social interaction or skill building. Time to Shop will help them transform the scene into a functional, adventure-filled role play.

ACTIVITY 12

Wrap It Up

FINE-MOTOR SKILLS

MATERIALS

- ○ Storage bins
- ○ Small boxes
- ○ Wrapping paper scraps
- ○ Gift tags
- ○ Tape (lots and lots of tape)
- ○ Scissors
- ○ Folder
- ○ Toy catalogs
- ○ Bows and ribbon

NUMBER OF CHILDREN AT CENTER

2 to 3

SETUP

- Place all the items in bins along the back of a work surface.
- Stack the boxes.
- Place the photographs inside the folder.

CENTER ACTIONS

Children find an item in a catalog that they would like to give to someone. They cut out the picture of the item and place it in a box. Now it is time to wrap it! Once the wrapping is complete, the children practice writing the name of the recipient on a gift tag. Then they get to deliver the gift to a friend or teacher. It is amazing to see the smiles on their faces when the recipient opens a pretend gift and shares excitement. Everyone loves opening presents, and teaching children to share the joy of giving gives them a lifelong social skill.

WHAT ARE CHILDREN LEARNING?

Children are working on many fine-motor skills in this center. They are using their fingers to wrap and tape their presents. They are practicing tying ribbons and writing names on the tags.

Children's imaginations are piqued while they work with the pretend gifts.

In the social arena, children are learning how to give. They are sharing emotions such as joy and excitement as they open their gifts.

ADAPTATION AND ENHANCEMENT IDEAS

Visit discount stores to purchase paper and bows. Inform fellow teachers, staff, and parents of this project. They can save small scraps of paper and old ribbons and bows for the activity. Buy extra tape and let the children have fun with it. It might take a recipient some time to get a present open, but it is worth the work.

ACTIVITY 13

Ice Cream, Ice Cream

LANGUAGE DEVELOPMENT

MATERIALS

- ○ Medium foam balls painted brown, white, and pink (for different flavors of ice cream)
- ○ Small foam balls painted red (for cherries)
- ○ Empty ice cream buckets
- ○ Colored paper
- ○ Empty whipped cream container
- ○ White felt, cut to resemble whipped cream
- ○ Small see-through plastic container
- ○ Ice cream scoops
- ○ Bowls and spoons
- ○ Menus
- ○ Empty chocolate syrup containers
- ○ Pictures of ice cream to color

NUMBER OF CHILDREN AT CENTER

4 to 6

SETUP

- Wrap each bucket with an appropriate color of paper and add a label.
- Make menus that replicate these labels.
- Put the foam ice cream balls in the correct buckets.
- Place the white felt pieces in the whipped cream container.
- Put the foam cherries in the small container.

CENTER ACTIONS

Children take turns being the workers and the customers in the shop. The customers look at menus and order their sundaes. The workers ask if they want one scoop or two, whipped cream, and cherries. While the customers wait for their orders, they can color the ice cream pictures. This keeps the customers engaged and not sitting idle while the ice cream workers are making the orders.

WHAT ARE CHILDREN LEARNING?

Children are practicing language and social skills when they interact with one another in this center. They are asking questions, taking orders, and using their memory to make the ice cream treats. Children can talk about flavors and how the ice cream tastes. They may show pride in the sundaes they make or exhibit disappointment if their ice cream rolls on the ground.

ADAPTATION AND ENHANCEMENT IDEAS

- Local ice cream shops may be willing to donate containers or posters to add to your shop. As a related activity, make real ice cream sundaes or banana splits as a special snack. The local shops might donate to this party.
- Have children decide on the sizes and colors of the foam balls when you are setting up the ice cream shop.
- Talk about how the foam feels, and invite children to color on it and try to cut it.
- They can dip the balls in paint and roll them on paper to create a unique design. Children can paint the balls and decorate the containers for the center.

ACTIVITY 14

The Mail Room

SOCIAL-SKILLS DEVELOPMENT

MATERIALS

- ○ Mailbox
- ○ Storage bins
- ○ Envelopes
- ○ Stickers to be used as stamps
- ○ Paper
- ○ Writing tools
- ○ Labeled photograph of each child
- ○ Folder
- ○ Mailbag
- ○ Play cash register with pretend money
- ○ Rubber stamp and stamp pad

NUMBER OF CHILDREN AT CENTER

3 to 5

SETUP

- • Purchase a child-sized mailbox, or make your own from a cardboard box painted blue with a flap cutout to put the mail in.
- • Place the different materials in bins at the center.
- • Place the labeled pictures of each child in the folder.

CENTER ACTIONS

Children take turns being postal workers and letter writers. Each letter writer draws a picture or writes a note, folds it, and places it in an envelope. Then the child addresses the envelope with another child's name (copied from the labeled photograph). Then it's off to the post office to buy a stamp! The letter writer puts the stamp on the envelope, and the postal worker stamps it with a rubber stamp and places it in the mailbox. Workers then collect the mail and deliver it to the correct people.

WHAT ARE CHILDREN LEARNING?

Children love getting mail and enjoy looking at the pictures from their friends. They work on social skills by saying "Thank you" to their classmates.

Children practice fine-motor skills when they draw, fold, and write names on their letters and add a stamp. They also use fine-motor skills when they try to put their letters in the envelope and use a sticker for the stamp.

As always when engaging in pretend-play scenarios, children are using language, asking and answering questions, and building vocabulary.

ADAPTATION AND ENHANCEMENT IDEAS

- • Children may want to use a tricycle or wagon for the mail truck to deliver the letters. This will add practice with gross-motor strengthening when they pedal the tricycle or push and pull the wagon. You could also decorate a large box for the kids to sit in for the mail truck.
- • Write real letters with the children. Have family members send the address of a grandparent, cousin, or other relative, and help the children write a letter or draw pictures to send to this special person.

ACTIVITY 15
Wash and Dry

FINE-MOTOR SKILLS

MATERIALS

- ○ Socks of different colors and designs
- ○ 2 large boxes
- ○ Empty detergent bottles
- ○ Clothesline or rope
- ○ Clothespins
- ○ Laundry basket

NUMBER OF CHILDREN AT CENTER

2 to 6

SETUP

- Decorate two boxes so that one is a washer and one is a dryer.
- Cut a door in each box that can be opened and closed.
- Tie the clothesline in a safe place where nobody will trip over it.

CENTER ACTIONS

Children practice the functional task of washing and drying clothes. Have the children put the socks in the washer and add the detergent. Once the wash cycle is complete, children can dry the socks in the dryer or put them in the laundry basket to hang on the clothesline. Once there, the children can find the matching socks and use the clothespins to pin them to the line. When the socks are dry, the children can fold them.

WHAT ARE CHILDREN LEARNING?

Children are working on matching skills when they sort the socks. They are working on fine-motor strength when they pinch the clothespins and pin the socks on the line. Learning about washing clothes, sorting, and folding is a life-skills lesson for children. They might even be able to help out at home the next time someone is doing the laundry.

ADAPTATION AND ENHANCEMENT IDEAS

- Clothespins can be painted so the children must match colors before pinning socks to the clothesline.
- Children can practice sorting skills by dividing all types of clothing into colors and whites or into items that can be worn in different seasons. You might have baby clothes, child-sized clothes, and adult items. See if the children can sort these or pick out the pieces they would wear. This is also a fun activity to do with mittens and gloves in the winter.
- Hang the clothesline over the water table. Put washcloths in the water and let children wring them out and hang the wet items up to dry. Talk about *wet* and *dry*, and have children predict how long it will take for the cloths to dry.

DRAMATIC PLAY AREAS

ACTIVITY 16

Pizza, Pizza, Pizza

SEQUENCING

MATERIALS

○ Cardboard
○ Silver paint
○ Velcro
○ Felt (brown, red, yellow, green, orange)
○ Empty cheese bags
○ Empty tomato sauce cans, other cans
○ Empty soda bottles
○ Paints and markers
○ Tagboard
○ Large box
○ Play cash register
○ Play money
○ Rolling pin
○ Pictures of pizzas to color
○ Oven mitts
○ Paper plates and cups

NUMBER OF CHILDREN AT CENTER

3 to 5

SETUP

● Cut a piece of cardboard into a circle to use for your pizza pan and paint it silver. Add Velcro pieces to each quarter of the pan. Glue brown felt onto another cardboard circle and cut it into four slices. This will be the crust that can be stuck onto the pan. The slices can then be easily removed when children are ready to serve the pizza.

● Fill the cleaned-out tomato cans and cheese bags, being sure all are free of sharp edges. Place red felt quarters into the tomato cans to be used as sauce. Cut yellow felt strips to place in the cheese bags. Green felt strips can be placed in a can with a green pepper label. You can do the same for the pepperoni. Be careful not to use too many toppings, as that can turn the pizza shop into chaos, with pieces being dumped out instead of being used functionally.

● Decorate the large box to become the pizza oven, and use the tagboard to make a menu for the pizza and drinks.

CENTER ACTIONS

Children take on the roles of customers, cashier, and pizza maker in this center. Customers study the menu and order a type of pizza and a drink from the cashier, who calls out the order to the pizza maker and collects the money. Then the pizza maker prepares the pizza: rolling out the dough, adding toppings, and putting the pizza in the oven. Customers color pictures while they wait, and the cashier serves them their beverages. When the pizza is done, the pizza worker uses mitts to take it out of the oven and puts slices on plates for the cashier to serve.

WHAT ARE CHILDREN LEARNING?

Children are participating in a dramatic play activity. They often verbalize their plan for play where they choose jobs and assign roles to each other. They may say, "I cook, and you order." They learn to take turns in the different roles at the center and practice courtesy and kitchen safety. They also practice sequencing when they do things in the correct order for each role. They are learning to ask questions as they take orders and to use their memories to make the correct pizzas.

continued

ADAPTATION AND ENHANCEMENT IDEAS

- Local pizza shops may be willing to donate pizza boxes, posters, or old menus to add to your center. You can paint pizza slices on aprons for the workers to wear.

- Post a picture sequence to help children learn the step-by-step process of layering the crust, sauce, and toppings. Expect children to sort the items back into the containers when they are finished.

- Children can help decide on pizza items they want in their shop. Bring out paper, felt, foam, and other materials for them to cut into shapes. Add silly items, such as carrots or jelly beans, and see what kinds of faces the children make when they pretend to eat and serve these pizzas.

ACTIVITY 17

Vet Clinic

REAL-WORLD ROLE PLAY

MATERIALS

- ○ Stuffed animals
- ○ Blankets
- ○ Tools from your pretend doctor kits
- ○ Bandages and wraps
- ○ Storage bins
- ○ Food and water bowls
- ○ Pet carriers, collars, and leashes
- ○ Shoe boxes

NUMBER OF CHILDREN AT CENTER

2 to 3

SETUP

- Find as many different stuffed animals as possible to come to school for their veterinary visits.
- Use real pet carriers, collars, and leashes for your center as you have children practice caring for the animals.
- Make up beds using shoe boxes and blankets or pieces of material.
- Sort the vet supplies into bins.

CENTER ACTIONS

Children take turns being concerned pet owners and veterinarians. The pet owners describe their pets' symptoms. Allow the vets to put bandages on animals and to wrap up "broken" bones with tissue or wraps. The children can use syringes, stethoscopes, and thermometers from play doctor kits to check on the health of each animal. This is an opportunity to talk about how to treat animals kindly and to be careful around animals they don't know.

WHAT ARE CHILDREN LEARNING?

Children are learning how to care for a pet. They are role-playing a real profession and seeing how different medical tools work for specific purposes. They work on language, as pet owners describing what is wrong with the pets and as veterinarians examining and treating the animals' different body parts.

ADAPTATION AND ENHANCEMENT IDEAS

- This is a great time to have a real veterinarian visit your classroom and talk to the children about the profession. A field trip to a pet store or a veterinary clinic is also fun during this center. (Be sure to ask about any pet allergies the children may have, and talk to the kids about the animals they will see and how to act around them.)
- Have children bring pictures of their pets from home to put on the walls of your clinic as decorations.
- Set up a veterinary zoo where children treat lions, tigers, and other wild animals as another center idea. This works well when a field trip to the zoo has been planned.

ACTIVITY 18

Baker's Work

REAL-WORLD ROLE PLAY

MATERIALS

- ○ Cookie sheets
- ○ Bowls
- ○ Spoons, whisks, and spatulas
- ○ Towels
- ○ Aprons
- ○ Play cookies
- ○ Measuring spoons and cups
- ○ Empty flour, sugar, and other containers
- ○ Cookie cutters
- ○ Timers
- ○ Pot holders

NUMBER OF CHILDREN AT CENTER

2 to 3

SETUP

- Commercial cookie cutouts, play cupcakes, and cakes can be purchased for this area. If funds for these materials are not available, make cookies out of paper or foam.
- To make an oven, use a piece of cardboard with a cutout door, and tape it over a shelf.
- Set timers so children know when their cookies are done.

CENTER ACTIONS

Children love to cook, and this center will allow them to use real cooking tools with which they practice baking. Children use spoons and cups to pretend to measure out and mix ingredients. They place the cookies on cookie sheets and put them into the oven. Be sure children use pot holders so they don't burn their fingers when taking the cookie sheets out of the ovens. Have them lift the cookies off the sheets with spatulas once the cookies have had time to cool. Exaggerated expressions of delight as you take a bite are always welcome, because the children will be excited to share a sample of what they have made.

WHAT ARE CHILDREN LEARNING?

Children are learning how to use tools that they may find in their homes while being introduced to basic kitchen safety. They are stirring, scooping, and mixing, so they can help the next time someone bakes. They are also practicing fine-motor skills when they try to balance a cookie on a spatula and transfer it from the cookie sheet and when they use pot holders to pick up the sheets. Many of the commercial baking products involve shape matching—for example, putting two cookie halves together or frosting the cupcakes.

ADAPTATION AND ENHANCEMENT IDEAS

- When this center is open and if you have a working kitchen available, it is always fun to make real cookies and bake them. Be aware of any allergies or food restrictions that your children have, and follow school policies when using raw materials.
- Cutting out chocolate chip shapes and gluing them onto a huge brown circle creates a classroom cookie that can be displayed in the bakery center.
- The clay or dough area can include cookie cutters and rolling pins to enrich the bakery theme.

ACTIVITY 19

Camp Out

REAL-WORLD ROLE PLAY

MATERIALS

○ Boxes

○ Paint

○ Metal rack or grate

○ Play food

○ Tongs

○ Tent (a pop-up tent that doesn't need stakes is best)

○ Sleeping bags

○ Pillows

○ Flashlights

NUMBER OF CHILDREN AT CENTER

3 to 4

SETUP

● Make a campfire out of cardboard boxes, and paint red and orange cutout pieces to represent the fire.

● Use another box for the grill. Add a cookie cooling rack on top of the box so children can put the food on the grill.

● Add tongs and play food, such as hot dogs and burgers, to the grill area.

● Have children help you put up the tent.

CENTER ACTIONS

Children can cook, tell campfire stories, and pretend to sleep in the tent as they enjoy the camping center. Children choose roles as they pretend to be the mom, dad, or child. They often include one child as a puppy or other pet along for the campout. Have them use tongs to move food on and off the grill and practice switching the flashlights on and off.

This activity also provides an opportunity to discuss fire safety.

WHAT ARE CHILDREN LEARNING?

Children are learning how to interact with one another in a pretend outside scene. They are learning about dangers, such as fire and grills, and how to be safe around them. They are also engaging in a camp scenario that many children may never experience in real life. You are providing them with a great adventure! Children who have camped before may bring their own ideas and past experiences to the center. This area often transforms into a raft trip or a safari as the play progresses.

ADAPTATION AND ENHANCEMENT IDEAS

● Make s'mores for snack by melting marshmallows in the microwave or using marshmallow cream with chocolate and graham crackers.

● Add music to this center with a camp song CD.

● Find a video on the Internet showing how to pitch a tent, and watch that prior to the adventure.

● Spread leaf cutouts around the room, and add a paper pond so children can walk through the woods and go fishing.

● Put stuffed animals—such as bears, squirrels, and birds—around the room and have students use binoculars to search for them.

● Weather topics also can be added to this center. One day, put a large rain cloud above the tent and see how the play changes.

ACTIVITY 20

Take Me to the Zoo

LANGUAGE DEVELOPMENT

MATERIALS

○ Boxes

○ Paint

○ Stuffed zoo animals

○ Labeled photographs of each animal (several copies of each)

○ Toy cameras

○ String or strips of paper

○ Construction paper

○ Zoo maps

NUMBER OF CHILDREN AT CENTER

6 to 8

SETUP

● Ask the children to help you paint boxes to use as the cages at the zoo.

● Cut a large opening on one side of each box so the children can see what is inside.

● Wrap string around the boxes to serve as the bars, or glue on strips of paper.

● Put the stuffed animals in their cages all around the classroom.

● Make a path out of construction paper with trails leading to the different animals.

● Create a map of the zoo, using pictures of the animals to show their locations, and make copies for the children.

● Give the copies of animal pictures to another adult in your building.

CENTER ACTIONS

Give each child a map and a camera. Have children cross off each animal as they come to it and pretend to take its picture. Collect the cameras and explain that the pictures will be printed for them to pick up. Later, direct the children to go pick the pictures up from the person with whom you left them. Have children use the pictures to practice learning the names of all the animals on their zoo trip.

WHAT ARE CHILDREN LEARNING?

Children are learning the names of different animals. They are following a path and using a map to find a location. These are all appropriate life skills they will use in the future. When they take pictures and go to pick them up, they will need to ask questions. This helps them become more confident when talking to adults. Encourage children to show emotions, such as excitement and fear, when they see the different animals. Talk about how they would feel if one of these animals came into the classroom.

ADAPTATION AND ENHANCEMENT IDEAS

● Instead of using cages, you can create a realistic environment for each animal. Put up paper trees in one area for the birds and monkeys, and use blue tissue paper for the water animals. Shred some green paper so the crocodiles or snakes can sneak through the grass. Rocks from outside can become mountains for the leopard to climb over.

● A trip to the local zoo is a great way to reinforce the discovery of animals and how we care for them. If that is not possible, you can go on a virtual trip to a zoo on the computer. Visit a national zoo website and look at the pictures of the different

continued

animals. Some zoos also have video cameras in some of their enclosures that show the animals in real time.

- Have children choose their favorite animals, and make a chart of their favorites. See if their favorites stay the same over the course of the school year.

- Children can be workers at the zoo and take groups of peers around to see the different animals. Help them learn animal facts to share.

ACTIVITY 21

Beauty Time

REAL-WORLD ROLE PLAY

MATERIALS

○ Wigs

○ Combs

○ Brushes

○ Hair clips, ties

○ Mannequin heads

NUMBER OF CHILDREN AT CENTER

2 to 4

SETUP

- Set aside an area in your classroom for a beauty salon.

- Provide mannequin heads with wigs on them for the children to comb, brush, and style.

CENTER ACTIONS

Lay down some ground rules about the wigs. Make sure children know that the wigs need to stay on the mannequins, so they are not putting them on each other's heads. Have the children practice combing hair and using their fingers to put clips and ties on the wigs.

WHAT ARE CHILDREN LEARNING?

Children are role-playing a career. They learn fine-motor skills when they use their fingers to manipulate the clips and ties. They practice conversational skills as they talk with other stylists and customers.

ADAPTATION AND ENHANCEMENT IDEAS

- Add old hair dryers or curling irons with the cords removed. Children enjoy pretending to make the noise of the dryers while they dry the hair.

- Add empty bottles of shampoo or hair gel to use in the shop.

- Include an appointment book and phone so customers can call to schedule appointments.

ACTIVITY 22

Little Builders

MATHEMATICAL CONCEPTS

MATERIALS

- ○ Toy or wooden hammers
- ○ Golf tees
- ○ Tape measures
- ○ Blocks of wood with predrilled holes (for golf tees)
- ○ Craft wood pieces with predrilled holes (for golf tees)
- ○ Large nuts and bolts
- ○ Toolboxes or shoe boxes

NUMBER OF CHILDREN AT CENTER

2 to 4

SETUP

- Borrow real toolboxes, or decorate shoe boxes to look like toolboxes.
- Have all tools and supplies in toolboxes in your center.

CENTER ACTIONS

For this center, you will need to supervise children closely and ensure that sizes of objects are appropriate for the ages of the children in your classroom. Have the children practice measuring with the tape measures and attaching the correct nuts and bolts together. They can use golf tees as nails to attach the different wood shapes to the blocks of wood.

WHAT ARE CHILDREN LEARNING?

Children are practicing numbers when they measure different items and learning concepts like *longer* and *shorter*. They are practicing fine-motor skills while learning how to use their fingers to hold a tee and hammer. They are matching nuts and bolts and using their fingers to screw them together.

💡 ADAPTATION AND ENHANCEMENT IDEAS

- Add small tool belts or nail aprons if you can find them.
- Show an episode of *Bob the Builder* to get children excited about the building center.
- Let children sand their wood pieces and paint them after they have nailed them together with the golf tees.
- Have children hammer the golf tees into pumpkins. Use a variety of colored tees so they can make designs.

ACTIVITY 23

Flowers for Sale

MATCHING

MATERIALS

○ Plastic flowers of different colors

○ Plastic vases and flowerpots of different colors

○ Pictures of different colored flowers on note cards

○ Small watering cans

○ Child-sized gloves

○ Little shovels and hoes

○ Sand or potting soil

○ Aprons

○ Dustpans and brushes

NUMBER OF CHILDREN AT CENTER

3 to 4

SETUP

- Gather materials during end-of-season clearance sales.

- Put pictures of different colored flowers on cards and place them on an empty toy shelf.

- Place the plastic flowers that match the cards on the shelf.

- Place a bucket with sand or potting soil in the area.

- Arrange the rest of the materials in an orderly way.

CENTER ACTIONS

The flower shop is a great social learning area where children can practice giving to others. Those who are workers wear aprons and take flower orders from the customers. Instruct them to talk about whom the cus-tomers are getting the flowers for and why: Is it a birthday? Is their friend sick? Customers should say what color flowers they want. Then workers find colored vases that match the selected flower colors. They put flowers in the vases and add sand or potting soil with their shovels. Customers can then deliver the flower creations to friends and teachers in the classroom. Of course, you need to be prepared for messes. Sand and soil spill and will cover the floor by the end of the day. Fortunately, children usually love to clean. Let the flower shop workers use dustpans and brushes to clean and tidy their work space before they leave.

WHAT ARE CHILDREN LEARNING?

Children are learning matching skills when they put flowers in matching pots and prac-ticing related organizational skills when they put the supplies away. They use memory to take orders and make bouquets. Functional skills are being practiced when the children sweep up messes and put items away in their spots. They are also learning how to share space and materials with other children, and they practice empathy when talking about the emotions associated with flower-giving occasions.

⋅◯⋅ ADAPTATION AND ENHANCEMENT IDEAS

- You can add a fun scenario by having other teachers call orders in to your room and allowing the children to deliver the flowers around the school or center.

- Include cards in the area and ask children to write a note to the person to whom

continued

they are giving the flowers. The child delivering the flowers might remember to say things to match the occasion, such as "Feel better!" or "Happy birthday!"

- Include pictures of flowers on the walls in this area and hang flower posters from the ceiling to add to the colorful scene.

ACTIVITY 24

All Through the Seasons

CATEGORIZING

MATERIALS

Fall
- ○ Leaves
- ○ Child-sized rakes
- ○ Pumpkins
- ○ Stuffed squirrels
- ○ Jackets

Winter
- ○ Foam snowballs
- ○ Sleds
- ○ Coats
- ○ Blankets

Spring
- ○ Flowers
- ○ Gardening gloves
- ○ Plastic bugs
- ○ Flowerpots

Summer
- ○ Beach blankets
- ○ Sunglasses
- ○ Caps
- ○ Seashells

NUMBER OF CHILDREN AT CENTER

4 to 8

SETUP

- Place distinctly seasonal items in the center, but do not sort them.
- Include clothing items that might be worn for each season as well as sports materials and other outdoor items.

CENTER ACTIONS

Children experience all four seasons in this center. They sort the items by season, deciding what to wear and which activities they would like to participate in. Children can talk about the weather in each season. Have them discover what happens if they wear a coat to the beach at the sand table or put seashells into a pile of fall leaves. Ask for their ideas about how each of the seasons makes them feel. (Sometimes it is exciting when it snows or sad if it is too cold to go outside.) Encour-age children to talk about different games, sports, or activities they can play in the different seasons, and recall season-specific holidays.

WHAT ARE CHILDREN LEARNING?

Children categorize items in many different ways in this center. They are also exploring environments and engaging in social interactions with their peers. They are talking to each other and deciding on scenarios to act out in the different seasons. If you live in a region that lacks diverse weather, this gives the children an opportunity to experience winter and sledding or fun at the beach.

⚙ ADAPTATION AND ENHANCEMENT IDEAS

- Add books about different seasons.
- Include stuffed animals that might be around during fall, winter, summer, and spring.
- Put in a plastic swimming pool and add seals and whales to watch from an igloo, or use it during the summer as a pool.
- Cover areas of the floor with different colored fabric for the seasons: brown for fall, white for winter, green for spring, and yellow for summer. Hang a sun, rain cloud, and snowflakes from the ceiling.
- If space is an issue, use materials for two different seasons at the same time, or put each season up one at a time. Add a funny item to each season to see if the children can figure out what is out of place, such as a stocking cap in the summer season or a sled in spring.

ACTIVITY 25

The Pumpkin Patch

SEQUENCING

MATERIALS

○ Plastic, cloth, or paper bag pumpkins with a hollow center

○ Velcro fasteners

○ Containers

○ Paper cutouts of leaves, eyes, noses, and mouths

○ Yarn (yellow and orange)

○ Pumpkin seeds

○ Cookie sheets

○ Plastic tweezers

NUMBER OF CHILDREN AT CENTER

3 to 5

SETUP

It is time to create a pumpkin patch right in your classroom!

- Look for plastic pumpkins after Halloween and take advantage of sales. Alternatively, paint paper bags orange or use cloth pumpkins in your patch.

- On each pumpkin, place Velcro strips where the eyes, nose, and mouth will go.

- In containers, sort cutouts of different shapes for these facial features, each faced with the other side of the Velcro.

- Cut yellow and orange yarn into three- to five-inch strips to put inside the pumpkins, and add real pumpkin seeds. (Make sure children know this is just for fun and they shouldn't eat the seeds in the play area. You may not be able to add seeds, depending on the ages, ability level of the children, and amount of supervision in your classroom.)

- Add plastic tweezers and cookie sheets to the center.

- Sprinkle leaf cutouts over the area, and place the pumpkins in the garden.

CENTER ACTIONS

Children visit the pumpkin patch and select a pumpkin. Then they clean out their pumpkins, using the tweezers to pull out the yarn and seeds. Have them separate the two, putting the seeds on cookie sheets to pretend to roast them. Next, children carve their pumpkin's faces, using the Velcro features. You might have some sample pumpkin faces up on the wall that the children can try to match, or encourage them to create their own faces. Talk about the emotions they can create on their pumpkin faces. What makes them feel happy, sad, or angry? They can also sort leaf cutouts into different shapes and colors and pretend to rake.

WHAT ARE CHILDREN LEARNING?

Children are learning to sequence when they pick a pumpkin, remove its insides, carve it, and roast the seeds. They use matching skills to make the faces and put their pieces away. They learn the labels for *eyes*, *nose*, and *mouth* and use sorting skills to separate the yarn from the seeds or to sort the leaves. They also use fine-motor skills to work with the tweezers. Children learn to play together in a dramatic play area.

continued

ADAPTATION AND ENHANCEMENT IDEAS

- A field trip to a real pumpkin patch can make this center come to life.

- Your class can also carve a real pumpkin and experience the different smells and textures.

- You can bring roasted pumpkin seeds for snacktime.

- Add costumes to this area so the children can dress up.

ACTIVITY 26

Going on a Trip

REAL-WORLD ROLE PLAY

MATERIALS

○ Chairs

○ Old cell phone

○ Cart

○ Snacks

○ Magazines

○ Tickets

○ Maps

NUMBER OF CHILDREN AT CENTER

8 to 10

SETUP

● Set up an airplane in your classroom by lining up chairs in rows. Have separate areas for the pilot and the flight attendant, placing the cart, snacks, and magazines in the flight attendant's area and using the cell phone as the pilot's microphone. Make tickets with colored shapes, and put matching colored shapes on the seats.

● Have the children look at maps and decide where they would like to travel to. If you have the resources, find cultural items from the place they select so the children can see these things when they arrive at their destination.

● Set up the items from the destination behind a bulletin board for the children to discover when they disembark.

CENTER ACTIONS

Children can gather at the center and decide who will be the pilot and the flight attendant. Have the flight attendant hand out the tickets to all the passengers, who then go to the dress-up area to put on outfits for the trip. Have them bring their tickets to the flight attendant when check-in is announced. Passengers must look for the correct seat and sit down.

During the flight, the flight attendant pushes around a cart with snacks and magazines. The pilot can announce the weather and arrival after the snacks are served. After landing, reveal any items from the destination for children to see.

WHAT ARE CHILDREN LEARNING?

Children are acting out occupations. They are using their imaginations as they role-play different scenarios and learn about new places in the world. They also develop conversational skills when they converse with the other passengers and the flight attendant.

ADAPTATION AND ENHANCEMENT IDEAS

● If children in your classroom have been on airplanes before, ask them to share their experiences and show photographs if they have them.

● Find pictures of airplanes or clouds and hang them from the ceiling over the airplane.

● You can show an in-flight movie for the children to view. Try to find one about airplanes or their destinations.

● Talk to the children about how crowded it is on the airplane. Passengers need to stay in their seats during takeoff and landing. They may need to get up and move if another passenger wants to get by. Teach them to use words like "Excuse me" and

continued

"Sorry" when they bump the chairs and move through the aisles.

- Add suitcases and ask children to pack items from the doll area or the kitchen to take along on their trip. See how they maneuver the cases through the tight aisles and pile them at the back of the plane.

Ask them to make their own tags for their luggage and attach those to every suitcase or bag.

- Use a program like Google Maps to show a satellite view of the route. You can zoom in on places the children may know.

ACTIVITY 27

Pet Care

RESPONSIBILITY

MATERIALS

○ Cage

○ Fish tank

○ Stuffed animals

○ Water bottles

○ Empty pet food containers (thoroughly washed)

NUMBER OF CHILDREN AT CENTER

2

SETUP

• Many schools (and some state regulations) do not allow living animals in classrooms because of children's allergies. If your program allows real pets, the children can have these experiences with a live animal. However, for this activity, you can use toy animals while still teaching children the responsibility of caring for a pet.

• Provide a hamster cage with a stuffed hamster or mouse.

• Include a fish tank with a stuffed fish or crab.

• In clearly marked areas, provide pet supplies, including the empty food containers.

CENTER ACTIONS

Ask the children to choose days when they would like to care for the animals. Be sure their responsibilities are clear to them. For example, the hamster will need the water changed in its water bottle, fresh food in its dish, and bedding changed in its cage. The fish will need food added to its tank.

WHAT ARE CHILDREN LEARNING?

Children are learning the responsibility associated with having a pet. They are taking care of their class animal and doing chores to keep their pet healthy.

ADAPTATION AND ENHANCEMENT IDEAS

• You can provide other pets that need care, such as a dog that needs to be walked on a leash each day or a bird in a birdcage.

• The pets could take turns going home with a child over the weekend or during breaks from school.

• Have children bring pictures of their pets from home to put up in the pet center.

• Talk to the children about how we know what our pets are feeling. Is the cat happy when she purrs? Is the dog angry when he barks, or is he excited when he wags his tail?

• Talk about animals that would not make good pets and why.

ACTIVITY 28
Cleaning Crew

REAL-WORLD ROLE PLAY

MATERIALS

○ Rags

○ Brooms and dustpans

○ Spray bottles

○ Wood chips

○ Plastic dishwashing basin

○ Plastic dishes

NUMBER OF CHILDREN AT CENTER

4 to 6

SETUP

Most children love to clean. Create a cleaning center around your sink area where they can explore these skills.

● Provide rags, brooms, dustpans, and toy vacuums for the children to use.

● Put dried wood chips on the floor.

● Place "dirty" dishes in the sink.

CENTER ACTIONS

Let children use the dustpans and brooms to sweep up the messes. Encourage them to pretend to follow the steps to wash and dry the dishes. Allow the children to spray water on the counters and clean them off. Talk about the opposites *clean* and *dirty* when children are participating in this center.

WHAT ARE CHILDREN LEARNING?

Children are learning how to keep their classroom neat and clean. These are skills they can use at home when they help their families do chores and share the responsibilities associated with maintaining a neat and clean household. Children are also using motor skills when they coordinate using a broom and a dustpan or carefully wash and dry dishes.

ADAPTATION AND ENHANCEMENT IDEAS

● If your classroom has jobs that the children choose, make cleaning one of the jobs. Children can clean the tables after snack or wash the dishes used during snacktime.

● Incorporate the idea of cleaning into the daily routine of your classroom to teach children responsibility and respect for their classroom and materials. They can help each other clean the centers before moving to other activities. Toys can be returned to shelves, and scraps of paper can be swept up at the art tables.

● Have cleaning supplies ready for the real messes that happen throughout the day. Sand may be spilled at the sand table, scraps need to be picked up at the writing center, and milk or juice often gets spilled at snack- or mealtime. Making cleaning materials available encourages children to be responsible for their own messes and take pride in having a neat classroom.

ACTIVITY 29

Pumpkin Wash

FINE-MOTOR SKILLS

MATERIALS

○ Toothbrushes

○ Small gourds or pumpkins

○ Trays

○ Towels

NUMBER OF CHILDREN AT CENTER

3 to 4

SETUP

● If possible, take children to visit a pumpkin patch and pick their own pumpkins.

● Set up the center with trays of water, toothbrushes, and rags.

CENTER ACTIONS

Have children put a pumpkin or gourd in the tray and use a toothbrush to clean it. While they practice scrubbing the gourds, they can discuss terms like *dirty* and *clean* and talk about the sizes and colors of the pumpkins. They will notice if some of them are smooth or bumpy and if their pumpkins are the same color or are mixed colors. Children should use towels to dry the pumpkins once they are cleaned.

WHAT ARE CHILDREN LEARNING?

Children are learning how to scrub and wash. These are skills they can use at home to rinse off plates from dinner and to scrub dishes. They are also drying their pumpkins, as they would dry off the cups or forks at home. Children will have a pumpkin to take home when they are done, and they can share the experience with their family.

ADAPTATION AND ENHANCEMENT IDEAS

● Children can paint their pumpkins or decorate them with art supplies once the pumpkins are dry. They can draw or paint faces on the pumpkins and talk about the feelings and emotions the faces show.

● The cleaned gourds can be used for size games or comparison activities.

● Experiment with different items for cleaning the pumpkins. Have children predict which ones will work better and try them out.

● Provide centers to wash other items, like apples. Choose foods you can serve for snack.

Soft and Creamy

USING THE SENSES

MATERIALS

○ Shaving cream
○ Paint shirts

NUMBER OF CHILDREN AT CENTER

3 to 5

SETUP

Shaving cream is a fun medium for children to explore.

- Be sure to find out if any children have sensitive skin and should not play with shaving cream. Ask if they can participate if they wear gloves.

- Set up the center on an easy-to-clean surface.

- Have children put on paint shirts or smocks to protect their clothing.

- Plan to be at the center or to have another adult there.

- Be sure no children put the shaving cream in their mouths.

CENTER ACTIONS

Have each child tell you a shape, number, or letter to make. Spray the symbol on the table, and let the children use their hands to spread it around. Some children may want you to spray the cream right into their hands. Children can draw with just their pointer, thumb, or pinkie finger to explore the medium further. Talk about the texture and temperature of what they are feeling. Talk about the noise the shaving cream makes when it comes out of the can. Provide a sink filled with warm water so children can wash their hands when they are finished at this area.

WHAT ARE CHILDREN LEARNING?

Children are discovering how to spread the cream around and draw pictures or designs. They feel it squeeze through their fingers and spread over the table. They also match their requests to the symbols you draw.

⚬ ADAPTATION AND ENHANCEMENT IDEAS

- Put the cream in a plastic bag and allow children to manipulate it in the bag instead of on a table.

- If you have a piece of Plexiglas, you can build a frame and base for it and mount it vertically. Children can stand one to a side. Spray the shaving cream on each side so the children can spread the cream away and peek at each other through the glass, or use a mirror and ask children to discover themselves as they wipe the cream away.

- Have children search through the foam to find beads or blocks.

ACTIVITY 31

Sensory Glurch

USING THE SENSES

MATERIALS

- ○ Liquid white glue
- ○ Liquid starch
- ○ Plastic scissors
- ○ Cookie cutters
- ○ Rolling pins
- ○ Trays

NUMBER OF CHILDREN AT CENTER

2 to 6

SETUP

Glurch is a sticky, smooth, puttylike medium for the children to feel and manipulate.

- Mix equal amounts of glue and liquid starch in a bowl with your hands.
- Add food coloring if you want specific colors to match the seasons or a theme.
- If the glurch is too sticky, add more starch. If the glurch is too stringy, add more glue.
- Place the glurch in a center at a table with the tools to use for exploring it.

CENTER ACTIONS

Give each child some of the material and tools to use in the exploration. Talk about how the glurch feels. Use terms like *wet*, *dry*, *cold*, *slippery*, and *sticky*.

WHAT ARE CHILDREN LEARNING?

Children are exploring with their senses of smell, sight, and feel. They are using tools to cut and press out patterns or forms. They can express themselves through a tactile medium.

ADAPTATION AND ENHANCEMENT IDEAS

- Glurch is one substance to use for sensory exploration. Other substances that are excellent for sensory exploration include gak, playdough, and oobleck. You can find recipes online for these and other substances. Try all of them, and see which ones engage the children.
- Add other tools and materials, such as plastic animals or blocks, to bury and dig out.
- Put different kinds of music on while children are playing with the glurch. See if the music makes them want to pound the glurch, stretch it out, or roll it into smooth balls.

ACTIVITY 32

Check It Out

EARLY LITERACY SKILLS

MATERIALS

○ Books

○ Pencils

○ Bookshelf

○ Blank cards for checkout slips and due-date cards

NUMBER OF CHILDREN AT CENTER

2 to 4

SETUP

Create a library in your classroom.

- Set aside a special space for bookshelves filled with interesting children's books.

- Place a checkout slip in each book.

- Set up a checkout desk for the librarian.

CENTER ACTIONS

Ask children to take turns being the librarian and the library visitors. When they find a book to check out, they can write their names on the cards and turn them in to the librarian. Allow the children to take a book home. Place the book in a plastic bag with a due-date card. They can bring books back and check out new books throughout the week.

Make sure children know how to act in the library. They should whisper to each other and move softly around the room. They may need to use a ruler to hold their book's place on the shelf in case they decide to choose a different one. You can specify the number of books they can check out.

WHAT ARE CHILDREN LEARNING?

Children are practicing writing their names. They are learning to enjoy and handle books carefully. They are learning responsibility by taking books home and bringing them back to school. They are learning how to act in a library.

ADAPTATION AND ENHANCEMENT IDEAS

- Visit a school or community library, or ask a librarian to come in to introduce this activity.

- Ask children to take turns with stories they like and pretend to read them to the other children who come in to check out books. Include beanbags and soft chairs in the area so children have a cozy place to read the books they have chosen.

- Staple or tape book covers to the wall of your library to highlight some of the children's favorites.

ACTIVITY 33

Fasten It

FINE-MOTOR SKILLS

MATERIALS

- ○ Coats and other clothing items with various fasteners
- ○ Backpacks
- ○ Bags with zippers

NUMBER OF CHILDREN AT CENTER

4 to 6

SETUP

This center focuses on a functional dressing skill.

- Set up an area in the classroom where children can practice working with many kinds of fasteners.
- Provide coats, backpacks, and bags with zippers for the children to work on.
- Include shirts and shoes with Velcro. Buttons and snaps are also found on many clothing items and can be included in this center.
- Real shirts can be used, or dolls and doll clothes can be added.

CENTER ACTIONS

Children use their fingers to zip bags open and closed, snap, and button. They can try on the coats and practice starting and pulling up the zippers. They can bring over their own backpacks or coats to the center and use them for practicing so they become more independent.

WHAT ARE CHILDREN LEARNING?

Children are working on fine-motor skills when they fit the zipper end in the correct spot and pull it up or put buttons through buttonholes. They are learning how different types of fasteners work so they know what to do when they encounter Velcro on a new pair of shoes or a snap on a coat. They may be able to help their friends fasten items when they are getting ready to go home, instead of asking an adult for assistance.

ADAPTATION AND ENHANCEMENT IDEAS

- Add backpack pulls to help children who don't have enough strength yet in their fingers to pull the zipper end. The pulls will allow them to hold something in their fist while pulling, which gives them more leverage and allows for independence.
- Place stuffed animals in the zippered bags for children to discover when they open and close them.
- Include other items with fasteners, such as shoes with laces, belts with buckles, or plastic bags that zip closed, for the children to explore.

Water and Sand Table Fun

USING THE SENSES

MATERIALS

○ A water/sand table from a school supply store or a large plastic container placed securely on a low table or bench

○ Plastic water shirts

○ See "Center Actions" section for items to place in the table

NUMBER OF CHILDREN AT CENTER

1 to 4

SETUP

The water/sand table is a must for any preschool room. Regardless of what is in the table, it always attracts the children. This is a place where they can play independently or in small groups.

● Rules for the table need to be established and should be posted with visual cues.

● Expect children to keep all materials in the table.

● Children need to wear plastic water shirts if there is water in the table.

● Inside voices must be used when playing at the table.

● Children are responsible for cleaning up any spills they make.

● Children should wash their hands before and after playing in the table.

● When small items are in the table, make sure you provide proper supervision.

● Change the items in the water table every week to keep the children excited about the area.

● Rotate between water and dry items.

CENTER ACTIONS

Here are just a few ideas for the water table. Use your creativity to think of more fun water table materials.

● Clean snow and mittens with little shovels and materials like wiggle eyes and buttons to make snowmen

● Ice cubes of different shapes or sizes

● Plastic fish or sponges

● Bottles, eyedroppers, and funnels

● Dirt with plastic flowers, trowels, and pots

● Ladybug counters or plastic worms

● Blocks with animals, counters, or people that go along with your book or weekly theme

● Strips of paper to make paper chains

● Beads and pipe cleaners or yarn to string

● Glurch (a mixture of equal parts liquid starch and glue)

● Cups and spoons for scooping and pouring

● Dry corn kernels

● Bubbles and bubble blowers

● Magnets

● Shaving cream

● Plastic bug counters with sand to sift

● Real seashells in sand

● Dishes and dish rags with soapy water for washing

● Plastic connecting toys or animals

continued

- Foam packing peanuts (*These are fun but often become full of static, so be aware of the need for cleanup throughout your room as the foam sticks to the children.*)
- Small apple or pumpkin cutouts and small pie tins (*Children can sort the cutouts and put them in the pie tins.*)

WHAT ARE CHILDREN LEARNING?

Children use their senses, their imaginations, and their curiosity to come up with all kinds of activities to enjoy. As they experiment, they learn about the properties of the items at the table, engage in conversation and play with others at the table, and enjoy self-directed learning. Table experiences are open ended and based on children's exploration.

ACTIVITY 35

What a Ball

GROSS-MOTOR SKILLS

MATERIALS

○ A variety of balls

○ Buckets

○ Baseball gloves

NUMBER OF CHILDREN AT CENTER

2 to 6

SETUP

- Create an area in the room or outdoors where children can play catch-and-toss.

- Include many different types and sizes of balls, such as tennis balls, softballs, basketballs, large therapy balls, Ping-Pong balls, and footballs.

- Set up baskets or buckets into which children can practice tossing the balls.

- Have baseball gloves for playing catch.

CENTER ACTIONS

Make sure children know the rules for throwing the balls in the area. Be sure to limit the number of children in the center to match available space. Encourage them to talk about sizes, colors, and textures of the different types of balls. Remind children to use the names of their friends ("Ready, Sam?") before they throw a ball.

WHAT ARE CHILDREN LEARNING?

Children are using gross-motor skills by throwing, catching, and making baskets. They are cooperating with friends when they toss the ball back and forth. They are learning to play with a partner and to focus on another child when they aim the ball to reach their friend. They are also discovering textures, sizes, weight, and colors as they play with their friends in this exploration area.

ADAPTATION AND ENHANCEMENT IDEAS

- Add an item that is not a ball to the center and see if the children can pick out the item that does not belong.

- Encourage the children to bring a ball from home and add it to the center.

ACTIVITY 36

Frozen Treasures

USING THE SENSES

MATERIALS

○ Ice cube trays

○ Small items to freeze in the trays

○ Containers to hold melting cubes

○ Container with warm water

○ Craft sticks

NUMBER OF CHILDREN AT CENTER

2 to 6

SETUP

This is a sensory activity and a scientific experiment.

● Freeze small plastic animals or other small items into ice cubes. Freeze a craft stick onto the top of each cube.

● Bring the cubes out during center time for the children to explore the sensory feel of the cold ice cubes.

CENTER ACTIONS

Place a small amount of warm water in a container along with the cubes. Encourage the children to move the cubes back and forth to melt the ice and discover the items that are frozen in the center. Ask the children to continue moving the cubes until all the animals are freed.

WHAT ARE CHILDREN LEARNING?

Children are experimenting with the way ice melts. They are using their senses to feel the ice cubes and to see how the water changes temperature when the frozen cubes are added. They practice prediction when they make guesses about what is hidden in the ice cubes. They check their predictions while a cube melts.

ADAPTATION AND ENHANCEMENT IDEAS

● Use ice cube trays in different shapes to freeze the items.

● Add food coloring to the ice cubes, and ask children to draw on paper with their frozen cube sticks. Watch how the food coloring transfers to the paper to make designs.

● Experiment with different ways to make the ice melt faster, such as placing it close to the heater or putting it into a microwave oven. Talk about why the ice melts more quickly in the heat.

ACTIVITY 37

Going Out

REAL-WORLD ROLE PLAY

MATERIALS

○ Fancy dress-up clothes
○ Ties, purses, jewelry
○ Mirrors
○ Shoes
○ Camera

NUMBER OF CHILDREN AT CENTER

2 to 8

SETUP

This center encourages children to engage in adult role play.

- Create a dress-up area and include items for a fancy night out.
- Place mirrors in the dress-up area so children can see what they look like.
- Put fancy dresses, suit coats, and dress shirts in a dresser or trunk for the children to discover. Include accessories so they can put on a tie or add jewelry to their outfits.
- Provide different shoes for the children to take out of boxes and try on with their outfits.

CENTER ACTIONS

Talk about how people act when they are dressed up to go out. Is it different from going to a ballgame or to the playground? Take photos of the children dressed up to go out and add them to your classroom photo album or computer blog. Parents will enjoy looking at pictures in the class album or during conferences. Add music so the children can go dancing and feel the movements with their grown-up clothes on. Do the clothes make it more difficult to move around?

WHAT ARE CHILDREN LEARNING?

Children are practicing being grown-ups. They are acting out scenes and using language skills to talk to their friends. They are working on dressing skills and developing fine-motor ability when they put on the different types of clothing and zip and button the items. Children are practicing manners as they ask for help, say "Thank you," and wait patiently for their peers to be ready. Children may pretend to hold a door open for a friend or help to fix a dress or scarf.

ADAPTATION AND ENHANCEMENT IDEAS

- Add a red carpet for the children to walk down.
- Make a large box into a car. Encourage the students to get into the car to leave for their night out.
- Use this area along with a restaurant theme in the kitchen area. Encourage children to eat out in their dress-up clothes, and encourage other children to act as cooks and waiters at the restaurant.

ACTIVITY 38

Punch It

FINE-MOTOR SKILLS

MATERIALS

○ Hole punches

○ Construction paper, patterned paper

○ Glue

NUMBER OF CHILDREN AT CENTER

2 to 8

SETUP

Set up a paper-punching center in the classroom. Include die-cut punches from scrapbooking tools, handheld punches, and many different colors and patterns of paper.

CENTER ACTIONS

The children use their fingers and hands to push down and squeeze the paper punches to make holes. Some children enjoy using their punches to make bigger projects, while other children just enjoy punching out the different available shapes. Provide construction paper so children can glue their punched shapes onto paper and make pictures, including collages.

WHAT ARE CHILDREN LEARNING?

Children are strengthening their hands and fingers when they press down on the punches. They are using the pieces they punched to create individual pictures on the construction paper. They are also learning how to use glue bottles or glue sticks.

ADAPTATION AND ENHANCEMENT IDEAS

● Add other art materials to the center for the children to use when making their pictures.

● Add scissors with different blade patterns for the children to explore while cutting.

ACTIVITY 39
At the Car Wash

FINE-MOTOR SKILLS

MATERIALS

○ Toy cars

○ Toothbrushes or cotton balls

○ Rags

○ Trays of soapy water

○ Box

○ Paper

NUMBER OF CHILDREN AT CENTER

4 to 8

SETUP

Have children run a car wash in your classroom.

● Prior to your car wash, schedule a day when the children can take the cars to the playground so the cars get nice and dusty.

● Prepare a box with a piece of shredded paper hanging from the top, both ends open, and a tray of soapy water outside it. This is the car wash.

● Provide toothbrushes, cotton balls, and small rags for use in scrubbing, washing, and drying the cars.

CENTER ACTIONS

The children run their cars through the box and into the tray of soapy water. They use the supplies to wash and dry the car. Then they line up the newly cleaned cars on the toy shelf for more driving fun. Note that there are many different aspects to this center for children to explore. They can be customers, washers, dryers, and clerks who collect money. They can work as a team to wash, dry, and line up the cars. Each child has a different job in the car wash line and trades jobs so everyone has a turn at each area.

WHAT ARE CHILDREN LEARNING?

Children are practicing fine-motor skills as they move the cars through the box and wash the dirt off. They learn and use vocabulary, including *clean*, *dirty*, *through*, *wet*, and *dry*. They also learn organizational skills when they line up the finished cars and sequencing when they move the cars through the car wash. They are learning how to play a role and complete a specific job to make the team run smoothly.

ADAPTATION AND ENHANCEMENT IDEAS

● On a nice day outdoors, have a bike wash or clean the riding vehicles from the preschool room.

● Place a small pool outside and wash classroom toys. Leave them outside in the sun to dry before returning them to the classroom shelves.

● Use the water or sand table as a washing area where children can clean blocks or plastic animals.

ACTIVITY 40

Story Box Treasure

EARLY LITERACY SKILLS

MATERIALS

○ Camera

○ Photo album

○ Treasure chest or decorated box

NUMBER OF CHILDREN AT CENTER

1 to whole class

SETUP

This is an activity that lasts all year and reinforces themes from stories you read to the children.

● Place a treasure chest in the story time area. In the chest place a photo album.

● Each time a book is read to the group, take a photograph of the story cover to add to the photo album in the treasure chest.

● Search around the classroom and find an item that represents each story. It can be something like a stuffed animal, a piece of food from the kitchen, a toy car, or an airplane.

CENTER ACTIONS

Encourage the children to decide on the item to go with each book. Place the item in the story box. Continue to gather items throughout the school year. Allow children to search through this treasure box and explore the items and photo album inside. When they visit the treasure chest, talk to them about what the items represent and help them remember the characters, plots, and adventures of the books read to them.

WHAT ARE CHILDREN LEARNING?

Children are making connections between representative items and stories. They can search through the treasure box during free-play time and rediscover some of their favorite stories. They can talk about what happened in the books and decide why they liked or disliked a particular story. Often stories are read only once. This activity provides a way for the children to revisit some favorites.

ADAPTATION AND ENHANCEMENT IDEAS

● Provide a treasure box for each unit that your class learns about. Place an item inside to represent each theme you do throughout the year.

● After you have collected several items, spread the photos out and see if the children can match the stories or units with the correct item.

● Use a treasure box in the classroom to collect a favorite item for each child in the room.

ACTIVITY 41

Magnets

SCIENTIFIC INQUIRY

MATERIALS

○ Magnets

○ Magnetic toys

NUMBER OF CHILDREN AT CENTER

2 to 6

SETUP

Create an exploration center with magnets. Include magnetized toys as well as objects that will be attracted to magnets.

CENTER ACTIONS

Children love to see how things stick together. Set the center up next to a metal file cabinet so children can attach the magnets to the cabinet. Include some fishing poles with magnets for hooks and items that can be picked up by the poles. Add magnetized wands to the center with paper clips or magnetic bingo markers that children can attract to their wands.

WHAT ARE CHILDREN LEARNING?

Children are learning about the science of magnetic attraction. They are experimenting to discover which items will be picked up by a magnet and which items are not attracted. They are also using materials cooperatively in a center where they need to share toys and work together.

ADAPTATION AND ENHANCEMENT IDEAS

- Encourage children to explore other items, predicting which will stick to a magnet. Provide a box with small magnetic and nonmagnetic items. Ask the children to use a magnet to separate the items into the two categories.

- Find magnetic puzzles to include in the area. These often include a fishing pole with a magnet for a hook to capture the puzzle pieces.

- Include pictures of all the children with magnets on the back. The children enjoy "capturing" their friends with their magnets.

ACTIVITY 42

Snow Cookies

USING THE SENSES

MATERIALS

○ Cookie sheets

○ Cookie cutters

○ Snow

○ Rolling pins

○ Spoons

○ Spatulas

NUMBER OF CHILDREN AT CENTER

2 to 6

SETUP

When you have a snowy day, collect some snow and bring it into the classroom for the children to feel and explore, focusing on making snow cookies. If snow doesn't accumulate where you live, you can make snow with a snow cone maker or ice shaver.

CENTER ACTIONS

Help the students scoop the snow onto the cookie sheets and use the rolling pins to press down the snow. Children cut out the cookies with the cookie cutters and use spatulas to move them onto a plate. See what happens when the snow begins to melt and their cookies turn into water.

WHAT ARE CHILDREN LEARNING?

Children are watching how snow turns to water when it melts. They are using their other senses when they feel the cold snow in their fingers and on their hands. They also employ pretend-play skills to roll out their snow cookies and use the cookie cutters and pans.

ADAPTATION AND ENHANCEMENT IDEAS

● Put snow in the water table with mittens so the children can play a frozen inside game. Add polar bear or penguin figures to the snow.

● Include sequins or buttons for the children to add onto their cookies as decorations. See if they float or sink in the water when the cookies have melted.

● Make real cookies for snack and add frosting and coconut sprinkles.

CHAPTER 3

Group Lessons

Group lessons (lessons that involve all children in the classroom) are a part of most preschool classrooms. By being involved in these lessons, children learn how to take turns and cooperate. Often, group lessons are part of the core learning area for skill development.

The activities in this chapter will help you think about *why* you are using an activity and *how* that plan will help children learn a skill. You will see opportunities to use group activities in four areas: to enhance academic growth, to improve social skills, to create hands-on learning experiences, and to promote musical creativity.

A key skill is highlighted at the beginning of each lesson guide, but the children's learning certainly is not limited to this skill. (See What Are Children Learning? in each lesson guide to get a sense of the richness of the lessons.)

Train Counters

COUNTING

MATERIALS

○ Boxes

○ Small objects

○ Paint and marker

SETUP

This is a hide-and-seek game during which children open boxes to find little treasures to count. It can also be played as a turn-taking game with the entire class or left in a center for individual exploration.

- Find small boxes, such as jewelry boxes.

- Paint each one a different color.

- Place small objects inside each box.

- On the bottom of each box, write the number that corresponds to how many objects are inside.

- Line up the boxes in a row to look like a train.

CHILDREN'S ACTIONS

The children each have a turn choosing which box they want to open by identifying the color. They open the box and count the objects inside. After they have counted, they can turn the box over to see if their number matches the numeral on the bottom of the box.

WHAT ARE CHILDREN LEARNING?

Children are learning how to count and match a number with the written numeral. They are also identifying colors as they choose the box they want to open. Concepts such as *open*, *first*, *last*, and *middle* can be reinforced as well.

ADAPTATION AND ENHANCEMENT IDEAS

- The items in the boxes can match the color of the box to reinforce color recognition and matching.

- The items can be categorical, such as foods, animals, blocks, or buttons.

- The items can be collected in a container. Then children can sort out the items into colors or categories.

- Remove all the box covers, mix them up, and ask children to find the matches and practice putting the covers back on the boxes.

- Place stickers or pictures on the boxes that focus on vocabulary and labeling.

ACADEMIC GROWTH

ACTIVITY 44

What Was That Sound?

LISTENING

MATERIALS

○ Plastic eggs

○ Small materials to go in the eggs

SETUP

This is an auditory matching game.

- Gather materials like pennies, cotton balls, beads, marbles, small wooden blocks, and bells.

- Fill pairs of plastic eggs with the same materials (two eggs with pennies, two with bells, and so on).

- Include two eggs that are empty.

CHILDREN'S ACTIONS

Children take turns shaking the eggs and trying to find a match based on sound. They can open two eggs when they think they have a pair with the same materials inside. Alternatively, give out all the eggs and ask children to find a partner that has the matching egg by shaking their eggs for each other and listening. Once children are paired up, let them open the eggs to see if they are right.

WHAT ARE CHILDREN LEARNING?

Children are learning to listen to sounds and discriminate among them, a key phonemic awareness skill. They are listening for matches and then visually discovering if they found the same or different objects.

ADAPTATION AND ENHANCEMENT IDEAS

- If it is too challenging for children to find the correct matches, limit the number of eggs available and make sure the sounds are quite distinguishable.

- Place opened eggs containing an item each in an egg carton, ask the children each to choose one, and then ask them to find its match by shaking the remaining eggs and listening to their sounds. This will help them learn how to match a visual to what they think its sound would be.

- Use small boxes instead of plastic eggs as containers and see how the sounds change.

Muffin Tops

MATCHING

ACADEMIC GROWTH

MATERIALS

- ○ Construction paper or tagboard
- ○ Markers
- ○ Pictures
- ○ Bowl
- ○ Wooden spoon
- ○ Tape

SETUP

This lesson will help the children learn how items are associated with each other. Pictures of associated items will be placed on paper muffin tops and muffin cups to make pairs.

- Make a poster out of construction paper or tagboard. Use markers to draw the muffin cups on the poster, and make the same number of unattached muffin tops. Draw enough cups so each child will have a turn.

- Find several pairs of pictures. Paste one picture on the muffin cup on your poster and the matching pair on the muffin top. For example, on one top you could have a bone and on the matching bottom a dog, or a train on the top and tracks on the cup.

- Place all the tops in a big bowl.

CHILDREN'S ACTIONS

Ask each child to come up and mix the "batter" with a wooden spoon. See if each child can reach in to scoop out a top with the spoon. Have children identify the items they pull out and tape them onto the matching muffin cups to create whole muffins.

WHAT ARE CHILDREN LEARNING?

Children are learning vocabulary words for the different items. They are learning how things are associated with each other. This lesson can use any pictures or vocabulary the children are working on.

ADAPTATION AND ENHANCEMENT IDEAS

- Use ice cream scoops and cones to find matching items.

- On the poster, provide the muffin cups and tops cut apart in a pattern so the children can self-correct by puzzling out which top fits into which cup.

- Use real muffin cups instead of a poster and tape the pictures on the cup. Ask the children to "pour" the matching picture in as the batter.

ACTIVITY 46

Glass of Milk

MATCHING

MATERIALS

○ Tagboard
○ Markers
○ Wooden craft sticks

SETUP

- Use a large piece of tagboard to make a poster.
- Make drinking glasses out of tagboard, drawing different shapes on each glass, and attach them to the poster. Mount the glasses on the tagboard so there is an open space at the top for a craft stick to poke out. On each craft stick, draw one of the shapes from the glasses.

CHILDREN'S ACTIONS

Ask the children to take turns putting all the sticks into the correct glasses so they look like straws.

WHAT ARE CHILDREN LEARNING?

Children are learning how to match shapes. They are using fine-motor skills to place the wooden straws in the correct spaces.

ADAPTATION AND ENHANCEMENT IDEAS

- This is another activity that can be changed to accommodate any lesson theme. For example, make each craft stick a different color and place different colored items to be matched on the cups—for example, red for apples and green for frogs.
- If children are working on letter sounds, write the letters on the straws and provide items with names starting with the letters on the cups.

ACTIVITY 47

Tops and Bottoms

COLOR RECOGNITION

MATERIALS

- ○ Construction paper
- ○ Scissors
- ○ Markers
- ○ Tape or Velcro

SETUP

- Cut several jack-o'-lanterns out of construction paper. Draw a face on each of them and color each nose a different color.
- For each jack-o'-lantern, cut a hat and a bow tie from construction paper that is the same color as its nose.
- Put paper cutouts of leaves all over the floor and line up the pumpkins in a pumpkin patch.
- Display the hats and bow ties in an area away from the pumpkin patch.

CHILDREN'S ACTIONS

Ask children to move through the leaves to the pumpkin patch and pick a pumpkin. They then bring the pumpkin to show their friends, and they must find a matching bow tie and hat. Talk about how the hat belongs at the top and the bow tie at the bottom when they attach these with tape or Velcro.

WHAT ARE CHILDREN LEARNING?

Children are learning the concepts *top* and *bottom*. They are doing color matching.

ADAPTATION AND ENHANCEMENT IDEAS

- Make pumpkins in different sizes and ask the children to sequence them from smallest to largest.
- Make the noses on the jack-o'-lanterns different shapes.
- Put patterns on the hats and bow ties and see if the children can find the patterns that match.
- Change the faces to match themes. For example, you can make clown faces for a circus unit.
- Make different types of hats and talk about the occupations that use those hats.

ACTIVITY 48

Daytime/Nighttime

SORTING

MATERIALS

○ Pictures of objects you would see during the day and objects you would see at night

○ Tagboard or construction paper

○ Tape, Velcro, or glue

SETUP

● Make one poster that is bright like daytime and one poster with dark colors to represent night.

● Find pictures of objects that would be seen in the daytime and others that children see at night.

● Daytime objects can include the sun, rainbows, a rooster, sunglasses, and school.

● Night things can include the moon, a bed, stars, bats, and owls.

● Include activities that might happen at both times, such as brushing teeth or reading a story.

CHILDREN'S ACTIONS

Have children take turns choosing a picture of a daytime or nighttime object and matching it to the correct poster. Once all the pictures are sorted, ask children to work together to create poster collages. The pieces can be glued on so the poster can remain displayed in the classroom, or pieces can be attached with tape or Velcro and taken off for another use.

WHAT ARE CHILDREN LEARNING?

Time is a difficult concept for many children. Young children may not be ready to understand *yesterday, next week*, or *in a month*, but they do understand *day* and *night*. Discuss words such as *light* and *dark* while teaching this lesson. After children have mastered the concepts of *day* and *night*, introduce *yesterday* and *tomorrow*. Continue to work with children to expand their understanding of time concepts.

ADAPTATION AND ENHANCEMENT IDEAS

● Challenge children by introducing them to nocturnal animals that may be new to them. Look these up on the computer, and talk about the new vocabulary.

● Talk about occupations that require workers to work at night, such as nursing or firefighting.

● This lesson can also be done with a summer and winter theme. Other opposites such as *wet* and *dry* or *hot* and *cold* can be turned into a learning game for the children.

Pie Count

COUNTING

ACADEMIC GROWTH

MATERIALS

- ○ Construction paper (several colors)
- ○ Paper cutouts, stickers, or die cuts of fruits and vegetables
- ○ Tape

SETUP

- Cut out pie tin shapes from different colors of construction paper. Make one for each child in your room.
- Put on a top "crust" that can be flipped up to see inside.
- On the inside, add visual representations of different numbers of apples, cherries, pumpkins, and so on.
- Write the corresponding number on the bottom of the pie tin.

CHILDREN'S ACTIONS

Let each child take a turn choosing a pie and identifying the color on the pie tin. The children then flip open their top crusts to discover what type of pie they have and then count the pieces inside. Ask the children to compare the number of pieces they counted with the number written on the bottoms of the pie tins.

WHAT ARE CHILDREN LEARNING?

Children are learning to count and to identify different fruits and vegetables in the pies. They are also practicing color and number recognition.

ADAPTATION AND ENHANCEMENT IDEAS

- Put silly things in the pies, such as worms or leaves, and see if the children would like to eat them.
- Make cakes the same way: children flip up the frosting to discover the flavor.

ACTIVITY 50

Push and Pull

GROSS-MOTOR SKILLS

MATERIALS

- Large boxes
- Obstacles like cones, furniture, or tape on the floor

SETUP

- Set up an obstacle course designed for the children to learn the concepts of pushing and pulling.
- They can push and pull each other from one cone to another.
- They can push and pull around a table or under a blanket held up by two teachers.
- Red tape can be placed on the floor, giving children a path to follow as they push their friend; use green tape for the pulling section of the path.

CHILDREN'S ACTIONS

Children work in pairs to move each other in a large box. Ask one child to sit in the box while the other pulls or pushes him along in response to your commands. Make sure children take turns so each gets to ride and to push or pull. Talk about the concepts of pushing and pulling while the children travel through the obstacle course. Add other concepts, such as *through*, *around*, *in*, or *between*.

WHAT ARE CHILDREN LEARNING?

Children are learning movement and location concepts. They are working cooperatively with their peers. They are also using gross-motor skills when they figure out leverage and how best to make the box move.

ADAPTATION AND ENHANCEMENT IDEAS

- Add pretend play to the activity. For example, encourage children to pretend they are horses pulling a wagon, a fire truck on the way to a fire, or a train heading for the circus.
- Add wagons or scooters to the pushing and pulling lesson. Talk about which items are easy to pull and which ones are more difficult.
- Ask the children to sit or lie on a blanket and hold on while another child tries to pull them on a smooth surface.

ACTIVITY 51

Apple Chart

GRAPHING

MATERIALS

○ Red, yellow, and green apples

○ Tagboard or construction paper

○ Many cutouts of apple shapes in red, yellow, and green

○ Marker

SETUP

● Make a blank graph with four columns.

● Use an apple cutout for each of the first three column headings—red, yellow, and green. Leave the fourth column blank.

● Place the graph on the wall in the snack area. Talk about apples as a fruit that comes in different types. Cut small pieces of the apples for the children to taste.

CHILDREN'S ACTIONS

After children sample the apples, ask them to report what color their favorite piece was. Have them pick apple cutouts that match their favorite flavors and put them on the chart. If some children do not like any of the apples, have them write an "x" in the fourth section. When each child has placed a cutout on the graph, count how many apples of each color the children liked. See which one has the most votes.

WHAT ARE CHILDREN LEARNING?

Children are learning how to graph items and vote for a favorite. They are counting and learning concepts such as *most, least, fewer,* and *more*. They are trying foods and discussing textures and flavors.

ADAPTATION AND ENHANCEMENT IDEAS

● Cut up the rest of the apples and put them together with some cinnamon and sugar. Cook and mash them into applesauce.

● Try this activity with different fruits to find the class's favorite.

● Offer different textures like soft marshmallows and chewy fruit snacks or different flavors like salty pretzels and sweet chocolate. Ask the children to vote for and discuss their favorites.

ACTIVITY 52

Sink or Float?

PREDICTING

MATERIALS

- ○ Clear bucket
- ○ Water
- ○ Objects to place in the water
- ○ Envelopes
- ○ Cards with pictures of the objects

SETUP

- During the classroom circle time, the children sit around a clear bucket or large clear container of water.
- Put two envelopes on the wall, one labeled *sink* and the other labeled *float*.

CHILDREN'S ACTIONS

Show objects one at a time to the children and ask them to vote on where to put the card for that item—in the *sink* or *float* envelope. Tally the votes and display the numbers. Talk to the children about which option has more votes, and put the card in that envelope. Choose a different child to place each object in the water to see if it sinks or floats.

WHAT ARE CHILDREN LEARNING?

Children are learning to make predictions and discovering if their predictions are correct. Teachers can talk to children about what the objects are made of and see if children start making connections between, for example, wooden pieces and floating or metal pieces and sinking.

ADAPTATION AND ENHANCEMENT IDEAS

- Encourage children to use toy boats to see if items that normally sink in the water instead float if placed on a boat.
- Allow children to look through the classroom to find items to experiment with.
- Expand this lesson to the water table. Include a variety of items that sink and float for the children to explore on their own or in small groups.

ACTIVITY 53

Feed the Bear

MATCHING

MATERIALS

○ Box

○ Colorful pictures of fruit

○ Glue

○ Furry fabric

○ Wooden block or cube

○ Paint

SETUP

- Paint each side of the block a different color so you can use it as a die. The colors should match the colors of the fruit in the pictures.

- Cover the box with the furry fabric.

- Cut a hole in the front for a mouth, and add eyes and ears so it looks like a bear.

- Scatter the fruit pictures around the room.

CHILDREN'S ACTIONS

Bring the bear out at circle time and tell the children he is hungry and hasn't eaten yet. Ask the children to take turns shaking the die. They can pretend to walk through the woods and find food for the bear that is the same color as their roll. They take turns identifying the food items and feeding them to the bear.

WHAT ARE CHILDREN LEARNING?

Children are building vocabulary when they learn the names of different fruits. They are learning colors and matching a color to an object.

ADAPTATION AND ENHANCEMENT IDEAS

- Give children directions to follow while they search for the fruits. For example, tell them to go *around* the table and *over* the blanket to a picture. This will help them work on listening skills as well as on following multiple-step directions.

- Read a bear story before you bring your furry bear out for the children to see, or make a different box animal to match your story.

ACTIVITY 54

Key Match

MATCHING

MATERIALS

○ Plastic keys

○ Cardboard sheet

○ Animal pictures

○ Shapes cut from construction paper (matching pairs of each shape)

○ Velcro

○ Bag

SETUP

● Make a board out of cardboard with ten windows that open.

● Place a different construction paper shape on each window and place a piece of Velcro on the front of the shape.

● Attach a matching shape to each key, with the other half of the Velcro on its back. Put all the keys in a bag.

● Hide a picture of an animal behind one of the windows. Tape the picture on the back of the cardboard sheet behind the window so it can be seen when the window is opened.

CHILDREN'S ACTIONS

Encourage the children to reach into the bag and pull out a key. Ask them to identify the shape and match it to the correct window. They then open the window to see if there is an animal hiding there. Continue giving children turns until the picture is found. Hide the picture again to give more children a chance to search for the item.

WHAT ARE CHILDREN LEARNING?

Children are learning to identify and match shapes.

ADAPTATION AND ENHANCEMENT IDEAS

● Spend time developing vocabulary by discussing the attributes of the hidden picture.

● Change what is matched—for example, colors, letters, and numbers. Hide letters and numbers behind the windows. When children find them, add them to a number line or alphabet chart to help children practice sequencing skills.

ACTIVITY 55

The Right Tool for the Job

MATCHING

MATERIALS

○ Outfits or hats that represent different occupations

○ Items that each worker would use on the job (for example: stethoscope, tape measure, hammer)

SETUP

● Set the workers' items in the back of the room.

● Choose one child to leave the room with an adult and dress up in one of the outfits or don the hat.

CHILDREN'S ACTIONS

When the dressed-up worker comes back in the room, ask the children to figure out what job that person would do. Ask the worker to choose another child to find a tool to fit that occupation. The second child goes to the back of the room, picks an item, and brings it to the worker. If the worker agrees, then the second child can leave the room for a turn to dress up. Put the clothing and items in the dress-up area for a week so the children can explore further. Talk about the occupations with the children, and have them share ideas about how each job helps people. See if any of the children's family members have the jobs you are discussing. If so, ask their children to share something they know about the occupation, based on observation.

WHAT ARE CHILDREN LEARNING?

Children are making associations between occupations and the tools that workers use in their jobs. Children are using dressing skills to put on and take off the clothing at the end of the lesson.

ADAPTATION AND ENHANCEMENT IDEAS

● Have children role-play something each worker does on the job.

● Take photographs of people in different jobs using a tool. Share and discuss the pictures with the children.

ACADEMIC GROWTH

ACTIVITY 56

Size It

CATEGORIZING

MATERIALS

- ○ Teddy bears in three sizes
- ○ Bowls in three sizes
- ○ Spoons in three sizes
- ○ Blankets in three sizes
- ○ Chairs in three sizes

NOTE: *The three sizes should be dollhouse-sized, child-sized, and adult-sized.*

SETUP

- Read or tell "Goldilocks and the Three Bears" to the class.
- Display the teddy bears at the front of the room.
- Have the other items stacked up beside you.

CHILDREN'S ACTIONS

Introduce the concepts of *small*, *medium*, and *large*. Talk about the bears and their sizes. Then have the children give the right bowl to each bear. Repeat with the spoons, blankets, and chairs. Talk to the children about other words that can be used for sizes such as *huge*, *tiny*, and *big*.

WHAT ARE CHILDREN LEARNING?

Children are learning to categorize items by size. They are also making a connection between the lesson and the story they heard. They are learning vocabulary words to identify the concepts of size.

ADAPTATION AND ENHANCEMENT IDEAS

- Ask children to find objects in the classroom for the bears and decide which bear is the right size for the item. Encourage children to talk about the items and what they are used for.
- Ask children to look at items of different sizes one at a time so they don't have other items for reference. Ask them to guess what size each item is. Then show them the other two objects and see if they change their minds with more information.
- Expand this activity to the kitchen area later in the day. Include the items used for circle time and let the children pretend with them, creating their scenarios with the materials.

ACTIVITY 57

Same and Different Match

COMPARING AND CONTRASTING

MATERIALS

○ Mittens

○ Two bags

SETUP

This game will help children learn about the concepts of *same* and *different*.

- Collect mittens to bring to school or use the children's.

- Put one mitten of each pair in each bag.

- You can either put matching mittens in the bags or mittens that don't match.

CHILDREN'S ACTIONS

The children can take turns picking one mitten out of each bag. Ask them to show the other children the two mittens, and talk about the concepts of *same* and *different*. When children pick a match, have them put the mittens on their hands. Keep going with this activity until all of them have found matching mittens. Encourage children to work on being supportive of one another. When someone completes a match, say, "You got it!" When the mittens don't match say, "Try again."

WHAT ARE CHILDREN LEARNING?

Children are learning the concepts of *same* and *different*. They can talk about the colors and designs on the mittens while they are finding the matches. They can work on expanding sentences and using parts of speech to tell their friends about their pairs of mittens.

ADAPTATION AND ENHANCEMENT IDEAS

- Ask each child to find one mitten hidden in the room and then search for the other child who has the match. These two children are then a mitten pair.

- Use socks to make matches instead of mittens.

- If you have a large group, you can limit the number of mittens to three or four pairs so the game does not become too long.

- Children can match actions while wearing their matching mittens. For example, pairs of children can stand face to face and mirror what their friends are doing with their bodies.

ACTIVITY 58

Where They Live

CLASSIFYING

MATERIALS

○ Playhouse

○ Play farm

○ Box with trees painted on it

○ Stuffed animals

SETUP

This activity will help children classify animals into categories of pets, farm animals, and jungle animals.

● Place the three models of environments (house, farm, jungle) at the front of the room.

● Hide animals throughout the classroom.

CHILDREN'S ACTIONS

At circle time, give each child a turn to search through the classroom to find an animal. When a child brings an animal to the front of the classroom, ask for the name of the animal and the child's guess about where the animal lives—house, farm, or jungle. Discuss the choice before the child places the animal in the correct environment.

WHAT ARE CHILDREN LEARNING?

Children are learning new vocabulary words to identify animals. They are answering questions when they share where the animal was found in the classroom. They are categorizing the animals based on where they live. Children may share other characteristics, such as what it says, its colors, its coat (scales, fur, hair), or its favorite food.

ADAPTATION AND ENHANCEMENT IDEAS

● Add other environments, such as water or snow.

● Include animals that can live in a variety of environments and see if the children want to include them in more than one spot.

● Count how many animals the children found for each area.

● See if the children can think of other animals that live in the same places.

Red Star Pictures

VOCABULARY DEVELOPMENT

MATERIALS

○ Pictures representing vocabulary words

○ Red marker

○ Photo album

SETUP

● Find pictures to represent vocabulary words you want the children to learn.

● Draw a red star on each of these pictures.

● Each day, hide a picture somewhere in the classroom for children to search for.

CHILDREN'S ACTIONS

You may want to assign a red star student each day to ensure that everyone gets a chance to search for a picture. When the picture is found, talk about where it was and identify the vocabulary word. Ask children to share what they know about the pictured item or concept. Use this time to expand vocabulary and sentences. Place the picture in a photo album in the book area each day so children can review the pictures they have found.

WHAT ARE CHILDREN LEARNING?

Children are expanding their vocabulary. They are using positional words, such as *under* the table, *in* the sink, or *on* the shelf, to describe where they find the picture. They are using sentences and expanding their understanding of items or concepts when they talk about the picture with each other.

ADAPTATION AND ENHANCEMENT IDEAS

● Make your pictures complement your theme for the week. A circus week, for example, should include pictures of animals, clowns, and a ringmaster.

● Find pictures that are unfamiliar to the children so they are expanding their vocabulary.

● Use pictures that illustrate actions as well as things, such as running, riding a bike, or playing together.

ACTIVITY 60

Interactive Bulletin Board

EARLY LITERACY SKILLS

MATERIALS

○ Tagboard

○ Construction paper

○ Velcro

○ Markers or crayons

○ Pictures

SETUP

Bulletin boards seem to be a staple in classrooms and throughout schools. Think about how you use bulletin boards: Are they interactive, or are they just pretty displays? Consider how you can make boards in your classroom interactive and promote learning. Use pictures to create a scene.

- Start with an empty board at the beginning of the month.

- At the bottom of the board where children can reach, place Velcro sentence strips: "I see ___." "I like ___." "I don't like ___."

- Create a word section with labeled pictures that match the main theme of your bulletin board.

- Attach a piece of Velcro to the back of each picture so the children can remove one and put it on the sentence strip of their choice.

- Every couple of days, add an element to the scene along with a new picture card.

CHILDREN'S ACTIONS

Children take a strip, add a picture card, and form a sentence. They may tell you, "I like pumpkins" or "I don't like spiders" or "I see the moon" as they observe these items go up on the board. Continue adding items until the end of the month, when you take down the board and start another.

WHAT ARE CHILDREN LEARNING?

Children are learning sentence structure. They are seeing written words that represent pictures and learning the left-to-right orientation of reading. They are interacting with the board and watching it change each day. Be sure to encourage the children to read the sentences aloud after they have created them.

ADAPTATION AND ENHANCEMENT IDEAS

- As children get used to the sentence strips, add descriptive words. For example, *big* and *little* or color names increase the length of children's sentences.

- Place a green "go" dot at the left edge of the sentence strips to help children orient their pictures from left to right.

- Be creative in what you add to your board. Staple on a real stocking cap for a snowman or use plastic flowers in flowerpots. This will keep your board exciting. When they see it changing, the children will continue to look for new items.

ACTIVITY 61

Fishing for a Friend

SOCIAL-SKILLS DEVELOPMENT

MATERIALS

○ Poster with a picture of a net

○ Metal juice or baby-food-jar lids

○ One picture of each student, teacher, and aide

○ A fishing pole with a magnet for a hook

○ Larger magnet

SETUP

This lesson helps children learn the names of their friends and teachers.

● Take photographs of all the children in your classroom as well as the teachers and aides.

● Glue each picture on a metal lid.

● In the middle of the net on the poster you have prepared, attach a magnet.

● Place the metal lids upside down on the floor so the images don't show.

CHILDREN'S ACTIONS

The children take turns using the fishing pole to catch one of their friends. When they have a friend on the line, have them identify the person they've caught. If they can, ask them to share something they like about that person. Then, place the metal lid onto the magnet in the poster, as if that person has been caught in the net.

WHAT ARE CHILDREN LEARNING?

Children are practicing the names of class-mates and teachers and learning how to compliment each other. This social game is a favorite and one that children will ask to play many times.

ADAPTATION AND ENHANCEMENT IDEAS

● Attach other items to the jar lids for children to fish for. Have children practice saying the names of colors, shapes, letters, or concepts on the jar lids.

● Use the fishing idea when children are picking friends to take a turn at different activities.

ACTIVITY 62

Smile, Please

SELF-AWARENESS

MATERIALS

○ Camera

○ Paper bags

CHILDREN'S ACTIONS

Most teachers use photographs in their classrooms. Here are some ideas on how to make your photographs educational as well as fun to look at.

Colorful Shots

Each child takes home a small paper bag and decorates it, using a specified color. Then the children bring the bags back, each containing an item of the given color from home. Encourage children to wear clothes that match the color. When they bring their items back to school, take each child's picture with the item. Put all the photos on a display board. (A child who does not bring an item to school can choose a toy from the room for the picture.)

Body Shapes

Have the children lie on the floor, forming different shapes or letters with their bodies. It is fun to get on a ladder and take the photographs from above.

Where Are You?

Work on positional concepts by taking pictures of children who have placed themselves somewhere. Have a child peek out from under the table. Take pictures of children standing and sitting. Form a line, and ask the first child or the last child to stand up. Encourage several children to pile into a tent to experience the concept of *full*. Label the pictures and put them in a classroom concept book.

Watch Us!

Use photographs to show families what their children are doing at preschool. Take action shots of children painting, looking at books, building, and climbing at the playground.

I Feel . . .

Take pictures of children with different facial expressions showing various emotions—for example, happy, sad, or frightened. Label the pictures and put them into a feelings book.

WHAT ARE CHILDREN LEARNING?

Children are using photographs to learn feelings, concepts, and colors. They are building vocabulary and sharing their school day with their families. The teachers are using pictures to help children learn about the world around them.

ADAPTATION AND ENHANCEMENT IDEAS

Consider creating a classroom blog. Viewing a blog is a great way for families to see what is happening in the classroom, access pictures, and find educational tips. Post pictures, classroom information, and tips on enhancing language, fine-motor and gross-motor activities, and social skills. Make sure you have permission from parents to use the pictures on the website, and follow any policies your school or center has for website postings.

ACTIVITY 63

The Circle Snack

SENSORY PERCEPTIONS

MATERIALS

- ○ Small plastic zipper food storage bags
- ○ Large bowl
- ○ Large spoon
- ○ Serving cups

SETUP

This is a snack lesson with a focus on sharing.

- Send home a small plastic bag with each child.

- Include a note asking families to send ½ to 1 cup of a circular food item.

- Offer ideas, such as cereals, round crackers, grapes, marshmallows, or raisins, if you think they're needed.

NOTE: *Whenever you are making a snack, make sure none of the children are allergic to food items that are included. Follow all school rules or policies that cover activities like this.*

CHILDREN'S ACTIONS

When the children bring in their items, ask them to tell what they brought, open their bags, and pour the snack into a large bowl. Talk to the children about where they got the items at home—Was the item in the refrigerator or a cupboard, or did they go to the store to pick it out? (Children like to hide their bags in their laps under the table and surprise their friends when it is their turn to share. Be sure to have extra bags of food in case a child does not come prepared.) When all the snacks are in the bowl, give each child a turn to mix with a spoon. Pour the snack mixture into cups and enjoy!

WHAT ARE CHILDREN LEARNING?

Children may try new foods. They can discuss the different tastes, textures, and whether they like or dislike them. They are learning to put things together and work as a group. This lesson also involves families with a school activity.

ADAPTATION AND ENHANCEMENT IDEAS

- If any of the children have severe allergies, work with the family on your snack idea. Families are often very clever when they have a child with allergies and can create a special pre-mixed snack to send along that follows your theme.

- Do a graphing activity after the snack. Make a list of all the items or tape one of each item onto a chart. Ask the children to come up and mark their favorite or least favorite item from the snack mix.

- Read a story about circles that complements the snack. You can even make this snack day a "Circle Day" by sitting in a circle for story time and making a collage using circle items.

- You can also use square- or rectangular-shaped snacks for this activity.

ACTIVITY 64

Hide-and-Seek Names

MEMORY

MATERIALS

No materials are required for this lesson.

SETUP

- This is a wonderful game to play during the first few weeks of school, when children are learning one another's names.
- Have one child step out of the room with an adult.
- Then choose another child to hide somewhere in the room. This may be behind a door, under a desk, or beneath a blanket.

CHILDREN'S ACTIONS

When the second child has hidden, the first student should reenter the room, look at the group, and try to figure out who is missing. Encourage children to use the name of the child who is hiding and to share something that child is good at, such as doing puzzles, sharing, or writing her name.

When children become accomplished at this game, they can recall details about the missing child. They might say something like, "It is the girl who has a green backpack and a sister named Sally."

WHAT ARE CHILDREN LEARNING?

Children are learning the names of their classmates, which will help them initiate peer interaction during playtime. It is fun when the teacher and other adults hide as well.

ADAPTATION AND ENHANCEMENT IDEAS

- If you have children in your room who have difficulty with language, make a folder with labeled pictures of each classmate and teacher. The child can then point to the missing classmate instead of answering verbally.
- Make sure the child who is hiding knows that it is okay to pop out, bounce up, and shout "Surprise!" when the seeker guesses correctly.
- See what happens if nobody hides or if more than one friend is missing.

ACTIVITY 65

Face It

EXPRESSING FEELINGS

MATERIALS

- Photographs of children expressing emotions
- Pictures of group scenes revealing emotions

SETUP

- Take photographs of children in your class with different expressions—for example, happiness, sadness, anger, tiredness, worry, and pain on their faces.
- In your group lesson, display the photos and the pictures of groups.

CHILDREN'S ACTIONS

See if the children can identify how the people in the group feel. Ask them to match that feeling to one of the photographs of a classmate. Be sure to validate each child's opinion because children may have different ideas about what is going on in the pictures than you do. Encourage sharing by all.

WHAT ARE CHILDREN LEARNING?

Children are making connections between feelings and the events that may cause them. They are sharing their ideas. You can encourage them to identify feelings when they play with friends throughout the day.

ADAPTATION AND ENHANCEMENT IDEAS

- Encourage the children to act out the scenes in the pictures, making the facial expressions they think fit.
- Encourage the children to move like they are feeling. How do they move if they are sad or excited?
- Include mirrors so children can see what they look like when they are experiencing different feelings.

ACTIVITY 66

Bless You

HEALTHY HABITS

MATERIALS

○ Construction paper or tagboard

○ Spray bottle filled with water

○ String

○ Tissue

○ Tape

SETUP

This is a social story that teaches children to contain a cough or sneeze.

- Construct a large doll out of construction paper or tagboard.

- Make a hole in the mouth big enough so the spout of the water bottle can be inserted in it from behind.

- Tape a string to the hand of the doll and run that up and through the mouth to the back of the doll.

- Put a crease in the doll's arm so it will bend.

CHILDREN'S ACTIONS

When the children join you at circle time, talk to them about sneezing and the importance of using tissues when they sneeze. Let them know that your doll friend has a cold and doesn't know the rules about covering her sneeze. Pretend to have the doll sneeze, and spray the water bottle. The children will see the sneeze go all over the room. Ask the children to come up with ideas about how she

can keep her germs to herself. Tape a tissue to her hand and pull the string from behind to pull her hand up to her mouth. Have her sneeze again against the tissue, and show the children how the germs are stopped by the tissue.

WHAT ARE CHILDREN LEARNING?

Children are learning how to keep their germs from spreading around the classroom. They are learning how to use tissues to keep the classroom a healthier environment. Talk to the children about using the inside of their elbows to smother coughs or sneezes when tissues are not available.

ADAPTATION AND ENHANCEMENT IDEAS

- Follow up this activity with a hand-washing unit.

- Make sure that tissues and hand sanitizers are available in the classroom, and encourage children to use them when they have a cold.

- Arrange for a nurse to talk to the children about germs and how they are spread to their friends and teachers.

- Include books about germs, doctors, and going to the hospital in the reading center.

- Set up a doctor's office in the dramatic play area.

ACTIVITY 67
Family Graph
GRAPHING

MATERIALS
○ Large poster board for graph
○ Markers
○ Small cutouts of boys and girls

SETUP
● Make numerous cutouts, using boy and girl outlines.
● Prepare a large graph with each child's name listed along the left-hand side (y-axis) and the terms *girls* and *boys* listed along the bottom (x-axis) in separate columns.

CHILDREN'S ACTIONS
Have the children talk about their family members and tell if they are boys or girls. (Decide whom to include: only people living in the home, pets, or extended family members.) Write the name of each family member on the cutout for that gender. Then complete the graph. Ask the children to put the girls in the "girls" column to the right of their names and the boys in the "boys" column. Count the number of girl and boy cutouts. Talk to the children about concepts such as *more*

and *less*. When all the children have taken a turn, tell them to look at the graph and decide whose family has the most members, whose has the most girls, and whose has the most boys. Count the total number of girls and boys for the children. Leave the graph up for several weeks and encourage the children to take turns sharing information about their family during circle time. Ask them to bring in photographs of their family members to share with the class when it is their turn.

WHAT ARE CHILDREN LEARNING?
Children are learning about their families and making connections to the gender of family members. They are learning how to graph and practicing counting skills.

ADAPTATION AND ENHANCEMENT IDEAS
● Make a family tree for each child. Place the boy and girl cutouts on or around a tree. Place apples on top of the cutouts with the names of family members.
● Introduce pronouns such as *he/she* and *him/her* during this lesson.

ACTIVITY 68

Dull Day Holiday

DEVELOPING MANNERS

MATERIALS

○ Small wrapped treats

○ Watercolor paints or markers

○ Pipe cleaners

○ Paper coffee filters

SETUP

● This is a social activity in which children move around the center or school to make deliveries.

● Prepare an art center where children can paint or use markers.

CHILDREN'S ACTIONS

Have children decorate coffee filters with the paints. Place a small treat in the middle of each filter, and wrap it with the filter. Use a pipe cleaner to tie the filter at the top. Give several of these treats to pairs of children to deliver to other teachers or office staff. Including an adult to travel with each group is a good idea to ensure that children are prac-ticing manners and politely addressing the teachers they are visiting. Children practice going up to classroom doors and knocking. Make sure they wait until someone answers the door before they go in. Ask them to share a special message and their treat with the teacher. This project can be used for "Happy May Day," "Happy First Day of Spring," or a spontaneous "Happy Thursday."

WHAT ARE CHILDREN LEARNING?

Children are learning how to approach a door and wait for a response. They are learning how to do something nice for another person and how it feels to share with others.

ADAPTATION AND ENHANCEMENT IDEAS

Ask children to make a special treat for differ-ent staff members for special occasions, such as birthdays or other holidays.

ACTIVITY 69

Penny Savers

SHARING

MATERIALS

○ Storage container

○ Pennies

SETUP

This is a giving activity. Children bring in pennies from home to contribute to a cause or charity. Each school year, choose a charity for your room to support. If one of the children in your room has a specific condition or disability, your class may choose to support a group for that cause. Keep a collection container in your classroom.

CHILDREN'S ACTIONS

Encourage children to bring in pennies from home throughout the school year. If possible, have someone from the charity come in to tell the children what the organization will do with their money. At the end of the year, have a celebration and count the pennies. Children can help stack pennies in groups of ten so you can put them into coin wrappers. If possible, have your class go on a field trip to turn in their donation.

WHAT ARE CHILDREN LEARNING?

Children are learning how to be supportive of a cause. Children are showing how they care about others and the community.

ADAPTATION AND ENHANCEMENT IDEAS

- Consider focusing the children's support on the local community. For example, a food bank or an animal shelter is an appropriate cause.

- Have a "Penny Day" each month to remind children to bring in their donations.

- Work at filling small containers. Dump those into the larger bucket when they fill up.

- Keep a supply of pennies for children who forget to bring theirs and those who can't contribute.

Feelings Video

SELF-EXPRESSION

MATERIALS

○ Video camera

○ Computer to collect images and format

SETUP

- Use a video camera to record different teachers in your building acting out scenarios that illustrate different emotions.

- Be sure your actors are aware of the purpose of the video and are expressive in the clips.

- It is fun to include children in this project, but you do need to be aware of any restrictions your center has on recording videos of children and showing them to other people.

CHILDREN'S ACTIONS

Show the recording to the children, leaving time after each clip to talk about the emotion displayed. Ask children to share their own ideas about the feeling—what caused it and how it was expressed.

WHAT ARE CHILDREN LEARNING?

Children are learning to identify emotions and to understand the relationship between scenarios and specific feelings.

ADAPTATION AND ENHANCEMENT IDEAS

Include still shots of people showing emotions. See if the children can guess the emotions that people are displaying. How does a person's face show an emotion? What about the rest of the body? Is there more than one emotion that fits a look?

ACTIVITY 71

Puppets Pop Up

PROBLEM SOLVING

MATERIALS

○ Puppets

SETUP

This is a discovery activity for the children to enjoy each day when they come into the room.

- Place animated puppets in different areas around the room.
- Pose each in a different location.

CHILDREN'S ACTIONS

The children may find the puppet sitting in the sink, holding a crayon at the art center, or reading a book. Put the puppet in situations that may be dangerous, such as climbing on a shelf, and see what ideas the children have to fix the problem. One day, the puppet can be surrounded by several toys that have been scattered around the room. What do the children think he should do about that problem?

WHAT ARE CHILDREN LEARNING?

Children will be excited to come into the room every day and see where their puppet friend is and what he is doing. They will be able to talk about the situations and brainstorm solutions to the puppet's problems.

ADAPTATION AND ENHANCEMENT IDEAS

Add a friend for your puppet to create social situations. Maybe one puppet is helping another at the cutting table. The two friends may have painted a picture together, or perhaps they are arguing. See if the children have any ideas about what may have happened and how they can solve the problem.

ACTIVITY 72

How Are You Today?

SELF-EXPRESSION

MATERIALS

○ Pictures depicting different emotions

○ Tongue depressors

○ Photographs of the children

SETUP

In this activity, the children share their feelings during circle time or at the beginning of their day.

- Prior to the lesson, give each child a tongue depressor to decorate.

- Add small pictures of the child at the top of the stick or write the child's name on the stick.

CHILDREN'S ACTIONS

When the children are gathered together, place the emotions pictures on the floor. Ask the children to choose a picture reflecting their feelings by placing their sticks under the appropriate pictures. Count how many children are feeling different ways, and see which emotion receives the most and the least votes. Ask children to share why they are feeling how they are.

WHAT ARE CHILDREN LEARNING?

Children are learning how to identify their emotions. They are talking about what makes them feel different ways.

ADAPTATION AND ENHANCEMENT IDEAS

- Make a bar graph to show the children's emotions. Use the pictures from the lesson on the sides, and stick the tongue depressors in rows to form the bars.

- Ask children to choose their emotions at the beginning of the day and then again at the end. See if their feelings change.

- Children can use a mirror to look at themselves to help them figure out which emotion to choose.

ACTIVITY 73

Get a Job

RESPONSIBILITY

MATERIALS

○ Poster with pictures of people doing different classroom jobs

○ Cards with each child's name and picture

○ Hole punch

○ Pipe cleaners

SETUP

Children love to help in the classroom.

- Separate children into groups—one group for each day they are in the program.

- Make a poster with pictures of different classroom jobs. Some ideas are line leader, turning lights off at the end of the day, cleaning the snack table, handing out snacks, and filling mailboxes. Limit the jobs each day to five main tasks so every child does not have a job every day.

- Bend small pieces of pipe cleaner and tape them to the job pictures as hooks.

- Prepare a card with each child's name and picture. (Color code the cards by day.) Punch a hole in each card.

CHILDREN'S ACTIONS

On their day, the children in that group will each have the opportunity to choose a job for that day. When they arrive for the day, lay out their name cards. Children take their own cards and put them on the hook next to the job they want to do that day. Then the workers get busy!

WHAT ARE CHILDREN LEARNING?

Children are learning how to help others and assist with needed jobs in the classroom. Having a job is a great way for children to learn responsibility. This activity will also help them learn the days of the week.

ADAPTATION AND ENHANCEMENT IDEAS

- Make job cards each week or month to match your weekly or seasonal themes.

- Change jobs periodically or add special assignments, such as taking an item to the office or a note to another teacher.

- Children typically are excited about having a job, and they keep track of what their friends have selected. Be sure to notice if children are choosing the same job at every opportunity. Make sure everyone gets a turn at a favorite activity; if necessary, remove that job for a few weeks so children must make different choices.

ACTIVITY 74

A New Friend

SOCIAL-SKILLS DEVELOPMENT

MATERIALS

○ Camera

○ Stamps

○ Envelope or postcard

SETUP

When families move or their situation changes, sometimes children join the program later in the year. Having a new person join the group can be scary and disruptive to the group and even more to the new child. As a teacher, you want to make this transition as smooth as possible.

CHILDREN'S ACTIONS

Prepare the group and the new arrival by using some of these tips.

- Share a photograph of the new child with your class.

- Take photos of the children in your class, the teachers, and the classroom centers. Send these to the new child so she has an idea about what she will be doing and who she will see when she starts school.

- Encourage family members to visit the classroom before the child starts coming to school so the family and the child can look around.

- Go to the new child's home for a visit before school starts so he can meet you and ask questions.

- Send out a letter or postcard telling the new child how excited you are to have her join your class. Give the child an idea of some of the activities the children will be doing on the first day.

- Invite the new child to bring family pictures or a favorite toy from home, for security.

- If the new child has a special need, talk to the group before the new child arrives and share information about the disability so the children can be prepared and comfortable. Encourage children to ask questions, and give them honest answers.

- Put the new child's picture up on the board and mark the day the child will start to get the group excited.

- Ask for a volunteer to be a buddy to the new child. The volunteer will help the new friend find things and navigate the schedule for the first few days.

- Encourage the children to send pictures or notes to the new child.

- Put up a map up in the room. Find and mark your city or town and the place from which the new child is coming.

- Talk to the group about the arrival of a new child and answer any questions they may have.

- Remind the children that the new child may need some time to learn the rules and routines. Everyone will need to be a little patient. Remind them of the first day they came to the center and how they needed to learn many new things.

- Ask the children to think about how the new child might be feeling on the first day and how the teachers may need to give that child some extra time to learn about the classroom.

continued

- Plan lessons and activities that encourage children to work together as well as small-group lessons so the new child gets to know her classmates in more intimate settings.

WHAT ARE CHILDREN LEARNING?

Children are learning how to accept new people into their classroom and routine. They are learning how to think from another child's perspective. They are learning how to be patient and share their own knowledge about school with newcomers.

ACTIVITY 75

Farm Scavenger Hunt

MATCHING

MATERIALS

○ Stuffed or toy farm animals

○ Two photographs of each toy animal: one black-and-white and one color

○ Poster board

○ Pictures of barns

○ Book about farms

○ Tape

○ Lists of where animals are hidden (for adult leaders)

SETUP

This lesson takes the children out of their classroom to explore your preschool or center.

● Make a poster with all of the black-and-white pictures of the animals, and display it outside your classroom door.

● Take the stuffed animals to different participating rooms in your building before the children arrive.

● Place a barn picture on the door of each room where an animal has been placed. This tells the children which rooms they can enter.

CHILDREN'S ACTIONS

Read a farm book to the children and tell them that all the animals from the book have escaped, and they need to help find them. Distribute the color photographs of the animals. Before the children go on the hunt, prepare each child to ask a question. (For example: "Do you have the horse?") Then organize the children in groups to search for their animals. Each group should have an adult leader. Make sure the group leaders have a list of where all the animals are hiding. Groups can go to many wrong places before finding the correct rooms. The children knock on the doors of classrooms with barn pictures and ask their questions. After the children have found their animals, they go back to their classroom and tape the color pictures on the black-and-white poster. The classrooms that they visit will love this activity almost as much as your preschoolers do. Other teachers will often create extra games and ask the children to hunt for other animals within the room. Make sure that the participating teachers put the animal in a visible place if they are not going to be present. It is disappointing when children cannot find a lost critter. Suggest that the animal be placed on the teacher's desk chair so children can easily find it resting there.

WHAT ARE CHILDREN LEARNING?

Children are learning about their preschool. They are asking questions and becoming comfortable with talking to other teachers. They are learning about animals that live on farms. This activity can also be done with zoo animals or house pets.

☀ ADAPTATION AND ENHANCEMENT IDEAS

● Plan an activity for the children when they return from their hunt. For example, put out farm puzzles to work on until all of the children return.

● If you are in a center that does not have other rooms, you can hide animals around the classroom. Children can ask questions, and you can give clues about where the animal is hiding.

continued

- Make sure children carry their photos when going to other rooms. At this age, some children may need to practice in a few rooms before they are comfortable asking their questions verbally. Don't push too much if they are reluctant to talk. You want this to be a positive experience, not a scary one. Usually by the time they reach the last few rooms, they are excited to go in and ask for the animals.

ACTIVITY 76

Focus on the Outdoors

MATCHING

MATERIALS

○ Camera
○ Computer and color printer
○ Paper
○ Crayons

SETUP

Nature walks are a nice way to get outdoors and to explore your center's environment and community. In this lesson, you will give the children a focus for their walk.

● A day before you take your group out, walk your planned route with your camera.

● Take pictures of items that you will see on the walk. These can be things such as a sign outside your center, a fence post, an unusual tree, or the slide on your playground.

● Size these photographs on the computer so that all of them will fit on a sheet of paper.

● Print enough sheets so each child can have one.

CHILDREN'S ACTIONS

When you are ready for your class walk, give each child a sheet with the pictures and a crayon. Ask the children to search for the items and circle each one when they see it.

WHAT ARE CHILDREN LEARNING?

Children are learning to be observant. They are also learning about part-whole relationships. They need to be outside exploring their environment and getting fresh air. In this lesson they are.

ADAPTATION AND ENHANCEMENT IDEAS

● On another outside walk, children can collect items. For example, give children a plastic bag each and ask them to find two leaves, a blade of grass, and a small stone. Then ask them to glue all these items onto paper when they return to the room.

● Take themed walks on which children look for things of a certain color or shape.

ACTIVITY 77

Box It In

IMAGINATIVE PLAY

MATERIALS

○ Various sizes of boxes

○ Art supplies

SETUP

There is some truth to the reports of people who say they buy expensive toys and the children end up playing with the boxes.

- Save boxes and encourage children to use their imaginations to decorate them, hook them together, or make them into a car or train.

- Different sizes of milk cartons make great building blocks. If you are extra ambitious, you can wrap the cartons with colored duct tape or construction paper.

- Boxes can also be turned into animals when you add some eyes, yarn for a mane, and clothespins for the legs or the feet.

CHILDREN'S ACTIONS

Include different sizes of boxes in a large play area and see how the children incorporate them into their play scenarios. The boxes may turn into hats or vehicles. Another fun activity with boxes is to give children two small boxes and ask them to stand with one foot inside each box. Turn on music and see if they can slide and skate around the room.

WHAT ARE CHILDREN LEARNING?

Children are learning to explore creatively. They are turning the boxes into whatever their imaginations can picture. They can use any art materials in your room to let their minds go off to magical worlds of purple painted cats or jeweled treasure boxes.

ADAPTATION AND ENHANCEMENT IDEAS

- Larger boxes can be used to make tents or forts, to turn into cages or lairs for stuffed zoo animals, or to create beds for kittens and puppies.

- Extra-large appliance boxes can be turned into cars, buses, igloos, and tree houses. Doors and windows can be cut out and paper tubes added so children can peek out through their binoculars. Felt and material scraps make good window coverings, blankets, and carpets.

ACTIVITY 78

Plant a Seed

SEQUENCING

MATERIALS

○ Seeds

○ Containers

○ Dirt or potting soil

○ Paper

○ Stapler

○ Watering can

SETUP

● Make a small book for each child by stapling several sheets of paper together.

● Prepare an area in which seeds can be planted and decide where the containers can be placed for students to observe over time. (Choose a sunny spot.)

CHILDREN'S ACTIONS

Help the children plant the seeds. Encourage them to experience how the dirt feels and to pick the seeds they want to grow. Ask them to draw pictures of planting for the first page of their book. Then they can draw the sequence of what occurs as they observe the plants growing. Children should care for their plants as well as observe them.

WHAT ARE CHILDREN LEARNING?

Children are learning what a plant needs to grow. They are learning the sequence of plant growth and documenting what they see happening in their books.

ADAPTATION AND ENHANCEMENT IDEAS

● If there isn't space outdoors to plant seeds, children can plant them in small clay pots in the room.

● They can make predictions about what they think their plants are going to look like. Add pictures of plants to your center or books about seeds and what they turn into. Maintain a collection of seeds and envelopes, and see if the children can match the seed to the flower or plant that it will turn into.

● Visit a farm, flower shop, or nursery to look at different plants. If you go after your classroom plants have grown, ask the children if they can find their plants in the shop.

● Be sure to know if any children have plant or pollen allergies you should be aware of before visiting a place like a flower shop.

Pop Pop

GROSS- AND FINE-MOTOR SKILLS

MATERIALS

○ Commercial or homemade bubbles

SETUP

● Watch for a nice day when children can enjoy playing with bubbles outside.

● Allow children to try blowing the bubbles themselves.

● Rounding their lips and creating controlled air flow helps them develop oral motor strength.

● Then watch them enjoy the bubbly experience!

CHILDREN'S ACTIONS

Encourage children to pop bubbles with different body parts. It is fun to see if they can pop bubbles with their elbow, nose, or a toe. Have them see how high a bubble will soar before popping. Ask children to work with partners to pop the bubbles. How will they move if they need to hold hands or keep their toes touching? Tell the whole group to hold hands and try to pop the bubbles with their feet or noses.

WHAT ARE CHILDREN LEARNING?

Children are practicing motor skills when they jump up to pop a bubble or poke one with a finger. They are also tracking with their eyes when they try to follow a bubble as it soars or drops down.

ADAPTATION AND ENHANCEMENT IDEAS

● There are newer bubble solutions available that stay formed longer. These are nice for children who have a difficult time moving their arms and hands quickly—they have more time to reach over to pop bubbles.

● Fill the water table with bubbles for a day and let the children explore that center on their own.

● Create bubble art by placing a straw in a glass filled with water, soap, and food coloring. Practice with the children first so they know how to blow and don't mistakenly drink from the straw. Encourage the children to blow bubbles into the glass through the straw. When the bubbles foam over the edge, lay a piece of white paper on top to soak up the color.

● Use a fan to blow the bubbles. Talk to the children about how the bubbles move differently and where the bubbles go in the classroom.

ACTIVITY 80

Beach Ball Bop

CATEGORIZING

MATERIALS

○ One or more lightweight, inflatable beach balls

SETUP

This lesson is a language game.

● Inflate the beach ball(s).

CHILDREN'S ACTIONS

Ask the children to stand in a circle. Pick a topic, such as animals, colors, vehicles, or body parts. Call out a child's name and toss her a beach ball. When she catches it, ask her to name something that belongs in that category. Then she picks a new person to toss the beach ball to. You can also make this a social game by encouraging children to share things about their friends while they pass the beach ball. Children can work in pairs to toss the beach balls back and forth instead of as a single group. Most children enjoy playing with beach balls, but some children are afraid of tossed balls. Allow them to stand back and watch if they are fearful and don't want to participate.

WHAT ARE CHILDREN LEARNING?

Children are learning to categorize. They are also practicing catching and throwing skills when they toss a beach ball back and forth.

ADAPTATION AND ENHANCEMENT IDEAS

● If a large play area is available, beach balls can also be used with rackets to practice tennis skills.

● Draw a face on a beach ball with permanent markers and put shaving cream on it for a beard. Children can use craft sticks to shave the beard.

NOTE: *This activity can be done with balloons instead of beach balls. Some states prohibit the use of balloons with young children. If your state permits the use of balloons, do not use them with children younger than three years old. Be aware that some children are allergic to vinyl and latex.*

Scarecrow Stuffing

FINE-MOTOR SKILLS

MATERIALS

○ Newspapers

○ Clothing items

○ Plastic pumpkin head

○ Camera

SETUP

Making a class scarecrow is a fun way to add a new classmate to your room.

● Save newspapers to use for this lesson.

● Collect items of clothing, including a hat, gloves, shirt, pants, and shoes.

● On the day of the activity, tear strips of newspapers for the children to crumple into balls.

CHILDREN'S ACTIONS

Children work together to crush paper into balls and stuff them into the pieces of clothing. They can identify the clothing items while they stuff them. When all the clothing is full, encourage the children to assemble their new classmate. They work as a team to put each item in the correct place, add more paper if needed, and fit the scarecrow together. Put the plastic pumpkin head on the top and add a hat to complete the project. Leave your new friend up in the classroom for several days. He can join story time, snack, and art projects. The children love having their picture taken with the friend. Make a scarecrow book with the pictures.

WHAT ARE CHILDREN LEARNING?

Children are strengthening their hands when they crush the paper into balls. They are working on identifying clothing pieces and body parts when they put the items together.

ADAPTATION AND ENHANCEMENT IDEAS

● Put the scarecrow in different places in your school or center. The children can discover him helping in the office or singing in the music area.

● If you have many costumes available, this activity can be completed by making a bear (or any other animal or character that matches your theme) to accompany a bear story or unit.

ACTIVITY 82

Hand in the Sand

SENSORY DEVELOPMENT

MATERIALS

○ Bucket

○ Sand

○ Blocks

○ Ping-Pong balls

○ Pennies

SETUP

- Fill a bucket with sand and hide several blocks, Ping-Pong balls, and pennies in the bucket.

- Keep one of each of the items out for the children to see.

CHILDREN'S ACTIONS

Each child will have a turn to find an item in the bucket. Have the children choose in advance which piece to search for. Each searcher reaches into the sand and feels around for the item. Once it's been found, the child places it with its match and chooses another child for the next turn.

WHAT ARE CHILDREN LEARNING?

Children are engaging in a sensory experience by searching through the bucket of sand and feeling for the shape of the objects they want to find. They are matching items when they find the correct pieces by using their tactile sense.

ADAPTATION AND ENHANCEMENT IDEAS

- Other materials that are fun to dig through are marbles, snow, and foam packing peanuts.

- Use small items that complement your theme. For example, use small plastic animals for a farm or zoo theme or hide seashells for a beach theme. Hide jewels in a treasure chest box and encourage children to become pirates seeking treasure.

ACTIVITY 83

Hatching

SEQUENCING

MATERIALS

○ Incubator

○ Duck or chick eggs

○ Heat lamp

SETUP

● Before you begin this project, make arrangements to send your hatched chicks to a family farm so you know the animals will have a good home when they leave your classroom.

● Research how to hatch chicks—there are many websites that provide information and lesson plans.

● You will need a source of fertilized eggs. You can order fertile eggs from a biological supply company, but these eggs don't always hatch. A local supplier may be a better source. Farm stores and pet stores may have information about a source for fertilized eggs.

● You will need to purchase an incubator. Many science education supply houses, such as Delta Education, Ward's Natural Science, and Discount School Supply, sell incubators. Once you acquire an incubator, follow instructions to set it up to hatch chicks or ducks. Incubators are fairly expensive, but one incubator can be used by several different classrooms year after year.

CHILDREN'S ACTIONS

Ask the children to check the eggs each day and watch for changes. They can keep a record book and draw what they are seeing. When the eggs hatch, you will need to keep the babies warm with a heat lamp and provide them with appropriate food and water. Ask the farm that takes the babies to photograph them in their new home and send the pictures to your group. Children can keep track of the chicks' progress in their books.

NOTE: *Some chicks usually die within days of hatching. You must be prepared for this possibility; some children may become very upset by the deaths.*

WHAT ARE CHILDREN LEARNING?

Children are learning to care for animals. They are discovering the sequence of an egg turning into a chick or duckling.

ADAPTATION AND ENHANCEMENT IDEAS

● Add books about chicks or ducklings to the classroom library.

● Take photographs of the eggs hatching into ducklings or chicks, or find pictures of the sequence on the Internet to share with the children. See if the children can put the pictures in the correct order.

ACTIVITY 84

Trim the Tree

FINE-MOTOR SKILLS

MATERIALS

○ Classroom tree
○ Ornaments

SETUP

● Set up a tree in your classroom around the holidays.

● If your center does not celebrate holidays, create a seasonal tree with leaves in the fall, snowflakes in the winter, and flower buds and birds' nests in the spring.

● Place ornaments for the tree at the front of the room.

CHILDREN'S ACTIONS

Ask children to take turns choosing an ornament for the tree. They can identify the color or design on the ornament and hang it on the tree. Vocabulary words to be used as they hang their ornaments include *top*, *middle*, *bottom*, *front*, and *back*. Tinsel and bows can be added to the tree. Include items that encourage children to work together, such as strings of beads. To hang these pieces, two or three children will have to hold the strings while moving around the tree to place the beads.

WHAT ARE CHILDREN LEARNING?

Children are working together to create a decorated tree. They are working on positional vocabulary words and labels for the items.

ADAPTATION AND ENHANCEMENT IDEAS

● Encourage children to make their own ornaments to place on the tree.

● Ask children to find specific ornaments. For example, ask them to find an ornament that is red, that is shaped like a circle, or that can fly to build comprehension skills.

ACTIVITY 85

Zoo Path

PREDICTING

MATERIALS

○ Pictures of animals (or stuffed animals)

○ Paper animal tracks or footprints

SETUP

● Make tracks for different animals that are found at the zoo.

● Tape them down on the floor in trails.

● At the end of each trail, hide a labeled picture of the animal or toy animal that matches the footprints.

CHILDREN'S ACTIONS

Ask the children to look at each set of tracks and guess which animal they think makes it. Encourage them to follow the trail and find the toy animal or picture to see if they are right. Then ask the children to talk about how the animal moves and pretend to be that animal as they move to the next set of tracks. Repeat this adventure until children have had a turn with each animal.

Children can complete this lesson in pairs. Partner work encourages children to talk to each other about the tracks and discuss what they find at the end.

WHAT ARE CHILDREN LEARNING?

Children are making predictions based on each trail of tracks they see. They are discovering animals and using gross-motor skills to act out how the animals move.

ADAPTATION AND ENHANCEMENT IDEAS

Encourage children to think by including unusual or unique tracks. Make a long line for a fish or a snake; create a section with no tracks and a crow or eagle at the end. Talk about what the birds' tracks would look like if they were walking on the ground. Make a track with many prints for a caterpillar.

Discovery Box

CATEGORIZING

MATERIALS

○ Box or trunk

○ Various items that fit into a category

SETUP

Keep a trunk or decorated box in the classroom somewhere. This is the discovery box.

• Fill the box with different items that fit a category. Change the contents of the trunk monthly or weekly.

• Initially, you may want to make a category obvious, such as yellow things, animals, or hats.

• As children improve using their classification skills, make categories more challenging, like things that are soft, have stripes, or start with the *b* sound.

• Allow children to play with the items in the box and use their imagination to see if they can find other connections.

CHILDREN'S ACTIONS

Place the discovery box in an area where children can explore it on their own or with peers and then use the materials during play. If you change the area frequently or regularly, the children will learn to predict when new items become available. On Monday morning, they will head over to make the discovery and encourage their friends to join them. As the categories become less obvious, they will engage in conversations to help them decide what the new category is. Always accept their answers, because they may discover a connection you did not think of. Take a picture of the items in the box each week for children to revisit in a photo book.

WHAT ARE CHILDREN LEARNING?

Children are learning how to classify items. They are learning to categorize and to see how objects fit together. They will also make up their own games and learning activities with the items available.

ADAPTATION AND ENHANCEMENT IDEAS

Add an item that does not fit the category, and see if the children can pick it out. Take a picture of that item and place it in an envelope on the box so the children can see if they found the right object.

ACTIVITY 87

Fishin' Positions

GROSS- AND FINE-MOTOR SKILLS

MATERIALS

○ Camera

○ Construction paper for fish cutouts

○ Paper clips

○ Fishing pole with a magnet for a hook

○ Photos of the children in different poses

SETUP

● Take photographs of the children in your class in different positions. They may balance on one foot, sit with their legs crossed, or have their arms over their head.

● Use a paper clip to attach the printed pictures to a cutout of a fish.

● Place all of the fish on the floor.

CHILDREN'S ACTIONS

Encourage the children to take turns using the fishing pole to catch a fish. They can remove the picture, show it to one another, and identify the pictured child. They then attempt to make their bodies match the position in the pictures.

WHAT ARE CHILDREN LEARNING?

Children are using fine-motor skills to attach the magnet at the end of the pole to the paper clip on the fish. They are using gross-motor skills when they use balance and coordination to match the body positions of their friends. They are also practicing social skills when they look at pictures of their classmates and identify who they are.

ADAPTATION AND ENHANCEMENT IDEAS

The pictures on your fish can be of anything that reinforces or enhances your theme or curriculum.

ACTIVITY 88

Find the Room

MATCHING

MATERIALS

○ Photographs or pictures of household items

○ Poster board

○ Bag for pictures

SETUP

• Make three small posters that look like different rooms: for example, a kitchen, bedroom, and bathroom.

• Find or take pictures of different items used in such rooms, like a pillow, toothbrush, or dishes.

• Place all of the pictures in a bag.

• During circle time, put the posters up on the wall.

CHILDREN'S ACTIONS

Ask children to take turns reaching into the bag and pulling out a picture. See if they can identify the object in each picture and place it in the correct room. Talk about activities that occur in the rooms. Ask children to think about when they spend time in the rooms, what they do, who is with them, and why certain activities can't be done in some rooms. Why can't they sleep in the bathroom or cook dinner in the bedroom?

WHAT ARE CHILDREN LEARNING?

Children are learning to make associations. They are learning new vocabulary words when they identify each item they take out of the bag.

ADAPTATION AND ENHANCEMENT IDEAS

Include other rooms, such as a garage or a laundry room. Extend the discussion to include inside and outside items and multiple-use items.

ACTIVITY 89

Make What I Make

FINE-MOTOR SKILLS

MATERIALS

○ Bowls
○ Blocks
○ Craft sticks
○ Small plastic animals or counters
○ Barrier

SETUP

● Give each child a bowl with some blocks, craft sticks, and plastic counters.

● Make sure all children have identically colored materials so each bowl is the same.

● Put up a barrier so children can't see what you are doing.

CHILDREN'S ACTIONS

Make something using some or all of the materials in your bowl. Show the children what you made and see if they can create the same design with their materials. Give them each a turn to make something for you and the class to copy.

WHAT ARE CHILDREN LEARNING?

Children are learning how to use their visual skills to match what they are seeing to what they are creating. They are using fine-motor skills to manipulate the objects and to place the items that match a sample.

ADAPTATION AND ENHANCEMENT IDEAS

● Remove some items from the bowl if the task becomes too difficult or frustrating.

● Add items that are more challenging to handle, such as round beads or tooth-picks, when the children become more skilled at this task.

● Ask children to watch you build the structure instead of hiding the building process so they can see how to place the items together.

ACTIVITY 90

What Sense?

SENSORY DEVELOPMENT

MATERIALS

○ Pictures representing the five senses

SETUP

- Create pictures that depict the five senses. Draw a nose, eye, ear, hand, and mouth or find a photograph or illustration.
- Post the sensory pictures in the classroom for quick references.

CHILDREN'S ACTIONS

When you are introducing new vocabulary words, help children learn to be aware of the different ways they can explore objects. Talk about learning new objects through the senses. Can an object be touched, smelled, seen, tasted, or heard? What do these different objects look like? Encourage children to use language to expand on their ideas. Discuss objects that can be observed by using the senses. Ask children to feel a cotton ball and smell it. Children can see a bell, hear it ring, and feel its smooth metal. Talk about why some items don't have sounds or why we shouldn't taste certain things.

WHAT ARE CHILDREN LEARNING?

Children are learning about their senses and how to describe objects based on these characteristics. This will help them expand their vocabulary and provide them with more descriptive words to use.

ADAPTATION AND ENHANCEMENT IDEAS

- Whenever possible, supply actual objects when introducing new vocabulary so the children can use their senses to explore and describe them.
- Devote a day to each sense. On hearing day, find things that make noises. On touching day, provide objects with different textures to explore. On seeing day, feature brightly colored items. Be aware of any children's allergies or sensitivities on tasting and smelling days.

ACTIVITY 91

Think Like a Scientist

PREDICTING

MATERIALS

- ○ String
- ○ Mittens
- ○ Blocks
- ○ Cotton balls
- ○ Glasses
- ○ Envelopes
- ○ Index cards or tickets

SETUP

For this activity, the children will be making scientific predictions.

- ● Set up three stations. Station 1: two pieces of string, one lying straight and the other forming a circle. Station 2: two mittens, one full of blocks and the other full of cotton balls. Station 3: two glasses of different heights and diameters.

- ● At each station, provide two envelopes, one for each of the two items.

- ● Give each child a card or ticket to use to vote for an item at each station.

CHILDREN'S ACTIONS

At each station, children will vote by placing their card or ticket in the corresponding envelope. At the first station, children can vote on which string is longer—the straight or circular one. At the second station, children can vote for the mitten they think has the greater number of objects in it. At the third station, they can vote for which glass they think will hold more water. When all of the children have voted, tally and report the votes. Show children the answers for each station by comparing the lengths of the strings, counting the items in the mitten, and pouring water into the two glasses. Discuss the answers with the children.

WHAT ARE CHILDREN LEARNING?

Children are learning to think scientifically. They are making predictions and testing hypotheses to discover answers. They are learning concepts such as *long, heavy, full, same,* and *different.*

☀ ADAPTATION AND ENHANCEMENT IDEAS

Find other items that can be compared and make more discovery stations. Scales for weighing, rulers for measuring, and containers for comparing volumes can be included to encourage children to explore properties of items and find answers.

Creepy Crawly Bug Hunt

CLASSIFYING

MATERIALS

○ Books and magazines featuring pictures of bugs

○ Magnifying glasses

SETUP

● Provide books and magazines in the reading area with photos and information about bugs.

● Provide each child with a magnifying glass.

CHILDREN'S ACTIONS

Encourage the children to read through some of the books and identify the different types of bugs they see. Ask them to count the legs and wings on the bugs and decide if each bug can walk or crawl. When children are done reading, give them each a magnifying glass and have them go outside to search for some real bugs. See what kinds of bugs they can find, and ask them to look closely at them with their glasses. When they are finished, ask them to describe the bugs they found. Be aware of any insect or outdoor allergies any children may have. Talk to children about insects that are not safe to get close to, such as bees or wasps.

WHAT ARE CHILDREN LEARNING?

Children are exploring nature closely and using their visual skills to search outdoors for insects. They are making connections between pictures in books and actual insects they see outside. They are using language when they talk about the names of bugs and what they do.

ADAPTATION AND ENHANCEMENT IDEAS

● When the children come back inside the room, ask them to draw pictures of the bugs they saw.

● Sing songs and teach children fingerplays about bugs.

● If you have any bug houses, collect a couple of bugs for the day and watch how they move before releasing them outside at the end of the day.

ACTIVITY 93

Musical Lights

SELF-EXPRESSION

MATERIALS

○ A CD or MP3 player and a variety of music (fast, slow, loud, soft, classical, and modern)

○ Flashlights

SETUP

- Cue up the music you want to play.
- Gather enough flashlights so each child has one.
- Turn the lights down and turn on the music.

CHILDREN'S ACTIONS

Tell children to move their bodies and their lights any way the music makes them feel. Encourage them to use language to talk about their feelings and how the music makes them want to move their bodies. Provide fast music, calming music, and music with strong beats. When a song is playing, ask children to point their lights up if they like it and down if they don't. Encourage children to share music or songs that they like. Ask them to name songs they enjoy hearing when they are sad or happy, and play those if you have them.

WHAT ARE CHILDREN LEARNING?

Children are expressing themselves through music. They are moving their bodies and using flashlights to display their movements. They are verbalizing their feelings and sharing their favorite songs.

ADAPTATION AND ENHANCEMENT IDEAS

- Offer children other objects to use when moving to music, such as scarves, instruments, streamers, or beanbags.
- Talk about the different patterns the flashlights make. See what happens when they all shine their lights on one spot. Tell them to make their lights travel in a path across the door frame or down a line on the ceiling, or direct them to use their flashlights to point at different items in the classroom.

Hands-On Fingerplays

ORAL LANGUAGE DEVELOPMENT

MATERIALS

○ Glove

○ Velcro

○ Felt

○ Scissors

SETUP

- Write down some of your favorite fingerplays.

- Make felt characters and pieces to go along with the fingerplays.

- Use an old glove and put Velcro pieces on the tips of the fingers.

- As you tell a fingerplay, add the felt characters to each finger to tell the story.

CHILDREN'S ACTIONS

Children will quickly learn the movements to the fingerplays and join in by making their bodies move to the actions. They will use expressive language to sing along with the rhymes. It is challenging for some children to both sing and perform the actions to the songs. They sometimes get caught up in what their bodies are doing and forget to sing along. They can combine the two skills after practicing.

WHAT ARE CHILDREN LEARNING?

Children are learning new songs using visual cues to help them remember the words. They can use the felt pieces on a flannel board to retell the story later, on their own or with their friends. They are using expressive language and memory to sing along with others and remember the words to the songs. They are using their bodies to move with the actions of the songs and are often isolating fingers or other body parts to complete the movement required.

ADAPTATION AND ENHANCEMENT IDEAS

- Make felt pieces to go along with other stories or songs. Use the glove, or make a felt apron for the pieces to stick to when you are sharing the story.

- Set up a flannel board in the classroom and turn on the music. The children can explore the pieces and set them up while the songs are playing.

ACTIVITY 95

Scarf Dance

SELF-EXPRESSION

MATERIALS

○ Scarves

○ A CD player or MP3 player and music with a variety of rhythms

SETUP

● Cue up the music you want to play.

● Give each child a scarf.

● Name the colors and the shapes of the scarves as you are handing them out.

● When each child has a scarf, turn on music with different tempos and beats.

CHILDREN'S ACTIONS

Tell children that they are going to move their scarves with the music. Encourage them to move around the room. Model how a scarf can move up, down, around, and under. Children can crawl, walk, or roll with their scarves. Allow them to move and express themselves in whatever way the music makes them feel. Ask them to share how they feel when the music is playing. Talk about the fast or slow tempo.

WHAT ARE CHILDREN LEARNING?

Children are expressing themselves and using a tool to show how they are feeling. They are becoming aware of their bodies and moving to different beats. They are moving around their friends and trying to fit into their own space in the classroom.

ADAPTATION AND ENHANCEMENT IDEAS

● Give one scarf to two friends and see if sharing it changes how the children move and what decisions they make.

● Tie a scarf onto a child's ankle or wrist so he doesn't have to hold the scarf while moving.

● Ask the children to share their ideas on how to move; encourage the whole group to mimic them.

ACTIVITY 96

Conga Line

GROSS-MOTOR SKILLS

MATERIALS

○ A CD or MP3 player and rhythmic music

○ Handheld musical instruments

SETUP

● Cue up the music you want to play.

● Give each child a musical instrument to hold and move with—maracas, tambourines, shakers, and bells are all good choices. Allow children to make their own selections.

CHILDREN'S ACTIONS

Play the music. The children can form a line and follow each other around the room to the beat of the music while playing their instruments. Give them a chance to be first in line and lead their classmates around the room. Allow them time to walk outside of the line and move freely to the music.

WHAT ARE CHILDREN LEARNING?

Children are learning how to be leaders and followers while they move around the room with their friends. They are also learning how to walk in a line. They are playing instruments and expressing themselves through movement.

ADAPTATION AND ENHANCEMENT IDEAS

● Encourage children to hold a toy animal and go on a musical zoo train.

● Give children a chance to explore many different tempos during your music activities.

ACTIVITY 97
Jukebox Rhymes

EARLY LITERACY SKILLS

MATERIALS

○ Cardboard or wooden jukebox
○ Old CDs
○ Pictures and printed nursery rhymes
○ Pennies
○ Paint
○ Scissors

SETUP

This activity gives children an opportunity to choose favorite songs from selections on a jukebox.

- Make a small jukebox out of a cardboard box, or have someone make you a solid one out of wood.

- Paint and decorate your box to look like an old-fashioned jukebox, leaving the top open to place the CDs in.

- Cut a small slit in the front of the box to drop pennies in.

- Cut another slot on the side so the children can pull out a CD after they have inserted their penny.

- Type the words to nursery rhymes and find pictures to help illustrate the rhymes.

- Glue the words on one side of an old CD and the picture on the other.

CHILDREN'S ACTIONS

Encourage the children to take turns putting in pennies and pulling out a CD. The group can recite the rhymes and participate with fingerplays and movement. Children are standing, sitting, and moving throughout this activity when they dance to the rhymes and come back to the jukebox for the next turn. This activity will keep children engaged and waiting for their turn to put in a penny. It is also a nice transition tool because it can be used as quick or lengthy activity, depending on the day's schedule.

WHAT ARE CHILDREN LEARNING?

Children are learning about visual representation through pictures. Nursery rhymes are a great way to practice memorization; children can go home and share the rhymes with their family. They are also exposed to rhyming, which is a fundamental skill in building language.

ADAPTATION AND ENHANCEMENT IDEAS

- Children can help create the CDs by choosing their favorite fingerplays and making the illustrations themselves.

- Use the same jukebox concept and put letters of the alphabet, shapes, or colors on the CDs. Pictures of favorite songs can also be used, which make it easy for children to select and listen to songs on their own.

CHAPTER 4
Arts and Crafts

Art activities are commonplace in most preschool classrooms, and there is no shortage of ideas for them. However, not all art activities are based on sound pedagogy. The art activities suggested in this chapter go beyond simple projects. They give children choices about what they want their work to look like and how they want to use the materials, thereby promoting discovery and creative learning. The lessons include ideas about how to use artwork to enhance other learning. The activities use typical preschool materials or household items that are inexpensive and easy to find.

This chapter presents the activities in two sections. The first is focused on Child-Centered Expressive Art ideas; the second emphasizes Creative Tools and Methods.

ACTIVITY 98

From Caterpillar to Butterfly

MATERIALS

- ○ Paint, including watercolors
- ○ Pom-poms
- ○ Pipe cleaners
- ○ Paper coffee filters
- ○ Brown paper bags
- ○ Wooden clothespins

CREATIVE PROCESS

Children will make a caterpillar that magically changes in its cocoon into a butterfly. Begin by reading a butterfly book to the children. Talk about how a caterpillar changes into a butterfly. Then head to the art table, where you have placed the materials. Tell children that they can use the materials to make caterpillars. Let the children choose paints, pipe cleaners, and pom-poms to use in making caterpillars. Tell each of them to paint a coffee filter with watercolor paints.

When the caterpillars are dry, carefully wrap them in their coffee filter blankets and place them in their cocoon bags. Then place the cocoons on a shelf in the classroom where they can be watched for several days. Be sure to regularly draw attention to the cocoons.

One day, after the children leave for home, tear open the cocoons and position each coffee filter into the clothespin to look like a pair of wings. Put the newly hatched butterflies all around the classroom. The children will be amazed when they walk in the next day.

Promote language by talking about where the butterflies are. Some may be high on the ceiling, at the bottom of the door, or in a corner of the room.

WHAT ARE CHILDREN LEARNING?

The children learn an important science lesson. They develop their fine-motor skills when they create their caterpillars. They may focus on color, answer questions, and work on concepts when they talk about where the butterflies have landed in the classroom.

ADAPTATION AND ENHANCEMENT IDEAS

It is possible to purchase a kit that allows children to watch a live caterpillar change to a chrysalis and then to a butterfly. Observing these changes and then releasing the butterfly into the outdoors offers a great opportunity to discuss the environment and nature.

ACTIVITY 99

Stuck on You

MATERIALS

○ Tagboard

○ Felt of different colors

○ All sizes, shapes, and designs of bandages

○ Glue

CREATIVE PROCESS

This is a traditional sticker activity with a twist. Children will use bandages instead of stickers to create their project. Children love bandages. They seem to be a cure-all for small scrapes and bumps. Somehow the act of putting on a bandage will make even an invisible sore disappear.

From tagboard, cut out large, 6 × 20 inch bandage shapes. Also prepare felt squares to glue to the middle of the bandages. Allow the children to choose which color pads they want and to glue them to the centers of their tagboard cutouts. Then they use their fine-motor skills to open the real bandages and use them to decorate the tagboard cutouts. When all the projects are finished, put up a bulletin board in the hall with the title "Stuck on Preschool."

WHAT ARE CHILDREN LEARNING?

Children are being challenged to peel the paper off the bandage and to stick it to the tagboard. They are building fine-motor skills.

ADAPTATION AND ENHANCEMENT IDEAS

- If the children have trouble getting the bandages started, flip over the corner of the backing paper so they have something to grab onto.

- Add bandages to the doctor center in your classroom.

- Talk to the children about what happens when they get hurt and need a bandage.

- Have them share times when they have needed medical care or have been in the hospital.

ACTIVITY 100

Gift of Time

MATERIALS

○ Photocopies of calendar pages for each month of the following year (one month per page)

○ Glue

○ Children's artwork

○ Yarn

○ Hole punch

○ Stickers

CREATIVE PROCESS

It is always a challenge to come up with gift ideas for family members. This is a gift that will last the whole year and be a keepsake for years to come. Children will each make a calendar to give as a gift.

In the fall, start saving special artwork that each child creates. Ask each child to help you choose twelve of the pictures. Try to include different media, such as paintings, tissue art, markers, and glitter. Print copies of the calendar pages for the next year and help children glue one picture on each month's calendar. Be sure to allow enough time, spreading the work over several sessions, because this is a time-consuming task. Have the calendars bound professionally, or just punch a hole through the pages and tie them together with yarn. Be sure to add a special sticker on each child's birthday and on the first day of preschool for the next year.

WHAT ARE CHILDREN LEARNING?

Children are using their fine-motor skills to complete the artwork for each calendar page. They are learning the art of giving and feeling pride in an accomplishment.

ADAPTATION AND ENHANCEMENT IDEAS

The children can use stamps or paint sponges to decorate their own wrapping paper. Then they can wrap their gifts for their families. Recipients often need to open their gift right away, because children are too excited to wait.

ACTIVITY 101

Jungle Zone Mural

MATERIALS

○ Jungle animal pictures

○ Paper

○ Art supplies

○ Computer and printer

CREATIVE PROCESS

Children will work as a group to make a class mural with a jungle theme. Create a jungle board in the shape of a tree and place it on a wall. Use cotton balls behind the leaves to make them three-dimensional.

Ask children to tell you what animals they would like to make. Assist them in looking up information and pictures on the computer of their chosen animals. Share some information about the animals and print one animal picture for each child.

Children can pick out materials from the art supplies to make their animals. Let them work freely. Ask them to tell you where to put their completed animals on the mural. Allow them to be silly and creative. For example, they may want to put the forest elephant in the tree or hang the tiger from a branch. You can also attach the computer pictures to the animals. Make sure both items go home with the children when it is time for the mural to come down.

When the mural is complete, ask the children to share their thoughts about how it turned out. Encourage them to use positive words to talk about the finished job.

WHAT ARE CHILDREN LEARNING?

Children are learning about being a part of something bigger than themselves when they contribute to the class mural. They are learning to be creative and they also are learning what real animals look like. They are learning how to access information on the computer and discovering that the Internet is a tool for finding answers to questions.

ADAPTATION AND ENHANCEMENT IDEAS

● Before you share what you have found about their animals, ask the children to tell you what they already know. You may be surprised. See if some of their answers match what you found on the computer and point out what may be different. Have a discussion involving other children by asking what they think.

● Other murals can be made: a farm, garden, or pumpkin patch. Let the children help you make the mural. Ask them for input and then follow their directions.

ACTIVITY 102

Hangin' Around Mobile

MATERIALS

○ Construction paper in a variety of colors

○ Art supplies grouped by color

○ Scissors

○ Stapler

○ Straws

○ String

CREATIVE PROCESS

Mobiles can be made to complement any theme or topic in a classroom. Creating this mobile will help children learn about colors.

Cut out various shapes—circles, squares, triangles, and rectangles—in different colors. For the mobiles to hang well, make the shapes approximately the same size. Allow children to choose their favorite colors, distributing four shapes of that color to each child. Encourage the children to use art supplies of the same color to decorate their shapes as they please. Staple two straws together at right angles in the middle to make an "X" for each mobile. Attach string to the ends of both straws with tape or staples. Attach a child's decorated shapes at the end of the strings. Add a string in the middle of the mobile to hang up the finished project. Suspend the mobiles from the ceiling in your classroom or hallway.

WHAT ARE CHILDREN LEARNING?

Children are learning and identifying colors and shapes. They are using their fine-motor skills to complete the project. As a class, the children are creating a rainbow of color in your room.

ADAPTATION AND ENHANCEMENT IDEAS

● Hang small signs with the names of colors in the areas where the mobiles are suspended, so children can make a connection between the written word and the color.

● Children can look for magazine pictures that match their color and glue those on construction paper to hang from their mobiles. Doing so incorporates practice in cutting skills. Alternatively, children can make letter mobiles from magazine pictures that match a letter.

ACTIVITY 103

Book-Craft Connections

MATERIALS

○ A favorite storybook

○ Art materials

CREATIVE PROCESS

Children love to listen to stories, and illustrating a scene from a story is a nice way to connect the domains of literature and visual art. When you are reading your favorite books to the class, ask children to think about the story and characters and how they might draw a picture of what's happening. Give them art supplies and see what they can make to go along with the story. Ask them to share their ideas. Print key words on the pictures they create.

WHAT ARE CHILDREN LEARNING?

Children are creating visual art that will enhance their understanding and knowledge of literature. While they are making their art project, talk to them about what happened in the story you read. They will use memory skills to talk about the characters, settings, and actions in the book. They are learning sequence when they share the plot and the chain of events.

ADAPTATION AND ENHANCEMENT IDEAS

● Hang the finished pictures in the hallway or hook them together and put the book in your classroom library.

● Keep a collection of the books that have been read and the children's visual interpretations of them.

ACTIVITY 104

Tissue Lights

MATERIALS

○ Tissue paper

○ Clear contact paper

○ Scissors

CREATIVE PROCESS

In this activity, children use contact paper and tissue to create a stained-glass window. Cut small squares of tissue paper and pieces of contact paper. The contact paper can be any size, depending on your project's theme and the available room for displaying finished pieces. Each child will need two identical pieces of contact paper. The children can help you peel the backs off their first pieces. Tape the sheets, sticky side up, by their corners to a table so the paper doesn't move and crinkle up. Ask the children to place tissue paper on the contact paper. They can use as many or as few pieces as they would like. When they are done, help them peel the back off the second piece of contact paper and place it over the first piece. The two pieces stick together with the tissue in between. Then the children can cut the contact paper into a shape or design. Hang their art from the ceiling or in a window so the light shines through it.

WHAT ARE CHILDREN LEARNING?

Children are using their fine-motor skills to peel the contact paper and to pick up small pieces of tissue to place on it. They are composing a finished piece by putting together smaller pieces in a pleasing arrangement.

ADAPTATION AND ENHANCEMENT IDEAS

• Use tissue in seasonal colors to go with the time of year.

• Children can add glitter or construction paper pieces to their art and observe how the light changes as it goes through the finished piece.

ACTIVITY 105

Farm Visit

MATERIALS

○ Camera
○ Art materials

CREATIVE PROCESS

After taking the children on a field trip, it is important to come back to school and relive the adventure through art. This lesson uses a farm field trip as an example, but any trip can result in an art creation.

Take the children on a field trip to a farm. Look at all the animals and watch their behavior. Talk about what the animals are doing and notice the colors and scenery around the farm. Take pictures of the field trip to hang up back in your room to remind the children of the animals, buildings, and machinery. If you can't go to a working farm, you can show a video about a farm. When the children return from the trip, provide them with art materials and ask them to make something that reminds them of their trip.

WHAT ARE CHILDREN LEARNING?

Children are using their memories to make connections between their trip and a creative project. They use what they learned on the trip and their imaginations to share their ideas and memories.

ADAPTATION AND ENHANCEMENT IDEAS

Let the children explain what their artwork is about and include what they say with their creations. This adds a language component to the lesson.

White to Bright

MATERIALS

○ White T-shirts
○ Fabric paints
○ Paint shirts
○ Sequins, plastic gems, or beads
○ Glue

CREATIVE PROCESS

Children will use their creativity to decorate a T-shirt to take home. Purchase T-shirts or have each child bring a white T-shirt from home to decorate at school. If the children prefer colored shirts, they can decorate those instead.

Children can use fabric paints to decorate the T-shirts. Allow them to mix colors, draw lines, or create scenes on their shirts. They can glue sequins, gems, or beads on their shirts if they want to add extra decoration. Make sure they wear paint shirts to protect their clothing while they are working. Take a group picture of everyone wearing their shirts when they are dry.

WHAT ARE CHILDREN LEARNING?

Children are engaging in creative expression by discovering how to use the fabric on their T-shirts. They will enjoy showing off their shirts to their families. They are also strengthening their fingers and hands when they squeeze the bottles.

ADAPTATION AND ENHANCEMENT IDEAS

● Hold a T-shirt day and ask all the children to wear the shirts they decorated.

● Ask children to decorate a hat or a bag in the same way, or ask them to each decorate a square of material. Hook all the squares together to make a class quilt.

Write a Book

MATERIALS

○ Paper (standard 8½ × 11 inch)

○ Stapler

○ Art supplies

CREATIVE PROCESS

This activity gives children an opportunity to write their own books. To make a small, eight-page book, cut a standard sheet of paper in half horizontally. Then put the two rectangular pieces together and fold them in half. Staple them together along the fold or spine of the book. Make a book for each child. Encourage the children to make up a story and draw pictures of it on their pages and decorate them. Then, while they are telling you about their stories, write down the words they use to describe each picture. Be sure to write exactly what each child tells you. It is important to validate their language and thoughts.

Put their finished books in the book area to be shared with classmates. They can take turns reading their books to the group during circle time or at the end of each day. When they do this, they are gaining experience in speaking publicly as well as sharing their imaginative ideas.

WHAT ARE CHILDREN LEARNING?

Children are learning how to put thoughts together and express them to another person. They are thinking about how characters and plot develop in a story. This is a fun activity to complete at the beginning of the year and again later in the year, to see how children's ideas change.

ADAPTATION AND ENHANCEMENT IDEAS

● Ask children to work in pairs. They can take turns creating the artwork and the narration. See if they can come up with ideas together.

● Add more pages for children who want longer books.

● Use larger sheets of paper if children want more room for the drawings in their books.

ACTIVITY 108

Blooming Artist

MATERIALS

○ Art projects from throughout the year

○ Camera

CREATIVE PROCESS

This is a yearlong activity that results in a display of each child's artwork. The actual displays typically take place during the second half of the year, after many projects have been completed.

Collect artwork from the children throughout the year. Ask them to choose the pieces they want included during the display week. Use a bulletin board space and give each child an opportunity to be the artist of the week. Ask the children to title their work, and take a photo of the artist to put on the board with the art projects. Put all of the collected artwork into a portfolio to send home with the children.

WHAT ARE CHILDREN LEARNING?

Children are learning to examine the work they have done and pick out favorite pieces. They are putting language to their art when they describe it or give it titles.

ADAPTATION AND ENHANCEMENT IDEAS

- If you have room, put the artwork up for all children in the class, creating a gallery of art they can share with other classrooms and families.

- Hold an art show for the families. Ask children to pass around cheese and cracker trays while the visitors look at the different art areas in the room.

Partner Art

MATERIALS

○ Art materials

○ Scissors

○ Glue

CREATIVE PROCESS

Creating art is often viewed as a solitary endeavor. However, many wonderful pieces can be produced when children work in pairs or small groups. Set out construction paper and other art materials, including scissors and glue. Draw names for partners or ask children to choose partners to work with.

The two children will go to the art area and decide what they want to make with the materials. Observe what the children discuss and how they decide what roles they will take. Does one child assign jobs like gluing or cutting, or do they negotiate for the jobs? Which materials do they choose to use in their project? Do they make something recognizable or more abstract?

WHAT ARE CHILDREN LEARNING?

Children are learning how to work with others. They are discovering what type of leaders they are and learning how to listen to their friends. They are deciding on a concept for their art.

ADAPTATION AND ENHANCEMENT IDEAS

- When it is time to take home the artwork, ask children to decide what they want to do with their piece. Do they want one child to have it, cut it in two, or take a photograph of it for each partner?

- Change the partnerships and see if the same children tend to be leaders or followers. Put two leaders together and see how that dynamic works. Provide projects for three children and observe those outcomes.

Disappearing Art

MATERIALS

○ Black construction paper

○ Snowflakes or ice cubes

○ A portable CD or MP3 player with music

CREATIVE PROCESS

This is a magical lesson that complements the weather. Take the children outside on a snowy day. Give each of them a piece of black construction paper. Play some music, and ask the children to move around, catching snowflakes on their paper. See what they create and how they move to the music. Bring the paper art indoors and see what happens when their creations melt. If you live where it does not snow, children can use ice cubes to draw on the paper and see what happens when it dries.

WHAT ARE CHILDREN LEARNING?

Children are learning creative expression when they move around to music and collect snowflakes. They are experiencing nature and observing the different patterns formed by the falling snowflakes.

ADAPTATION AND ENHANCEMENT IDEAS

● Ask children to use white or other colors of paper and see what works best to view the snowflakes.

● Bring a dish of snow into the classroom and watch what happens as it warms up.

● Complete experiments to see what melts faster: snow that is spread out or snow compacted into a snowball. See what happens when the snow is put next to the heater or in the microwave.

ACTIVITY 111

Body Outlines

MATERIALS

- ○ A roll of craft paper or newsprint
- ○ Markers, crayons, and colored pencils
- ○ Art supplies, including material, yarn, and buttons
- ○ Glue
- ○ Scissors
- ○ Mirrors

CREATIVE PROCESS

Children will make and decorate life-sized outlines of themselves. Have each child take a turn lying down on a large sheet of paper. Encourage them to arrange their arms and legs in an interesting position and trace around the whole body with a fat marker.

Provide art supplies and ask children to decorate their outlines. They can add material and buttons for clothing and yarn for hair, making their outlines three-dimensional if they choose. Talk about emotions while they draw facial details: How will they show themselves feeling? Why? You can provide mirrors for them to use, so they can see what they look like and attempt to recreate their appearance.

WHAT ARE CHILDREN LEARNING?

Children are thinking about their physical and emotional selves while they work. They use fine-motor skills to add items and color to their self-portraits.

ADAPTATION AND ENHANCEMENT IDEAS

- Ask children to practice labeling the different body parts on their outlines.
- Encourage the children to pose their outlines at the snack table, by the computers, and playing with toys. Take photographs of the outlines in different areas of the room.

ACTIVITY 112

My Beautiful Face

MATERIALS

○ Mirror

○ Washable markers

○ Rags

CREATIVE PROCESS

Children are practicing drawing skills as well as learning about facial expressions in this lesson. Ask children to look at themselves in a mirror. A standing mirror or a mirror hung on the wall works best; children can take the time to study themselves without another person having to hold the mirror up for them.

Give the children washable markers and let them draw their faces on the mirror. When they are done, or if they want to change something, they can wash the mirror off and create a new image. Encourage children to display different emotions, such as sadness, anger, or excitement in their drawings.

WHAT ARE CHILDREN LEARNING?

Children are practicing drawing skills. They see what different facial expressions indicate about feelings. They are learning about body parts and including parts they may not typically think about when drawing pictures of themselves without the mirror present.

ADAPTATION AND ENHANCEMENT IDEAS

● Use full-length mirrors, and ask children to draw their whole bodies, or have a partner help them.

● Ask students to copy the drawing on the mirror onto paper.

ACTIVITY 113

Around It Goes

MATERIALS

- ○ Barn cutout made from construction paper for each child
- ○ Paper circle for each student, sized to fit behind the barn cutout
- ○ Art supplies
- ○ Glue
- ○ Scissors
- ○ Brad fasteners
- ○ Farm animal stickers, cutouts, or pictures

CREATIVE PROCESS

Children will make a paper barn with a spinning wheel on the back that reveals the animals through the barn door when it is turned. Provide children with the barn cutouts. Ask them to decorate the barns with paints and art supplies. They can use markers to draw windows or a roof. Direct them to cut out a door at the bottom of the barn (you may need to model this) and to also cut out the spinning wheels. The children then put animal stickers, animal cutouts, or pictures of animals from a magazine around the wheel.

Help them attach it to the back of the barn with a brad fastener. This wheel can then be turned to view the different animals through the barn door.

WHAT ARE CHILDREN LEARNING?

Children are learning about farm animals while using their creativity to decorate a barn. They are choosing which animals to display in their barns. They are practicing fine-motor skills while cutting, gluing, and drawing.

ADAPTATION AND ENHANCEMENT IDEAS

- Use the barns and spinning wheels while you sing "Old MacDonald Had a Farm" at music time.
- Make use of the wheel concept for other themes. For example, a face can incorporate a wheel with different mouths showing different emotions. An ocean scene can include a wheel with different types of sea life.

ACTIVITY 114

Cocoa Bear

MATERIALS

○ Bear outlines

○ Glue

○ Paintbrush

○ Spice bottle filled with cocoa with holes in the top

CREATIVE PROCESS

In this activity, children will use not only their inventiveness but also their sense of smell. Provide different outlines of bears for children to choose. Allow children to color their bears if they want to. Then have them use paintbrushes to spread glue over their bears. When the glue has been applied, they can take the spice bottle and sprinkle cocoa over it. Tell children to hold their bears over the trash can to shake off excess cocoa. Be sure they smell their bears once they're done and the glue has dried.

WHAT ARE CHILDREN LEARNING?

Children are using their senses to smell the cocoa. They are deciding where to spread the glue and how much cocoa fur they want to shake on.

ADAPTATION AND ENHANCEMENT IDEAS

● Provide hot chocolate for snacktime to see if cocoa tastes like it smells.

● Children can use coffee grounds to make brown bears or white cocoa for polar bears.

● Experiment with other ground spices with strong aromas, such as cinnamon, nutmeg, cloves, and ginger.

ACTIVITY 115

Beach Scene

MATERIALS

○ Paper

○ Glue

○ Paintbrush

○ Sand

○ Shells

○ Sea life pictures

CREATIVE PROCESS

Summer at the sandy beach is the theme for this art project. Give each child a piece of paper. Have them spread glue around the paper with a paintbrush. Let them sprinkle sand over the glue. Encourage children to feel the sand on their hands and fingers before putting it on the picture. Children can also add seashells or pictures of sea life or sand creatures, such as crabs and turtles, to add to their artwork.

WHAT ARE CHILDREN LEARNING?

Children are feeling sand in their fingers and experiencing the sensory input. They are learning about different environments.

ADAPTATION AND ENHANCEMENT IDEAS

● Children can complete this project wearing sunglasses, as if they were at the beach.

● Put all of the pictures together to make a large beach. Ask children to paint a large sheet of paper blue for the ocean, and add fish and other sea creatures to the water.

ACTIVITY 116

Squishy Butterflies

MATERIALS

- Large sheets of paper
- Permanent marker
- Fingerpaints
- Spoons
- Paint shirts
- Glitter

CREATIVE PROCESS

To complete this project, children will press paint between papers to create unique designs. Use the permanent marker to draw outlines of butterflies on large sheets of paper, enough so every child can have one. Ask children to put on paint shirts to protect their clothing. Give them spoons and tell them to scoop out paint and drop it onto half of their paper. Then they should fold the paper in half and start pressing it together, causing the paint to spread. As they work, ask them if they can see the paint spreading around the paper, and find out their ideas about what their pictures will look like when they open them. When the children are done pressing, ask them to open their papers and see what they have created. They can add glitter while the paint is still wet.

WHAT ARE CHILDREN LEARNING?

Children are creating projects that will all turn out differently. They are using their fingers to spoon paint onto their papers, and they learn about the concept of *half*. They are using muscles to press the paper and spread the paint out. They are observing the geometric principle of reflection.

ADAPTATION AND ENHANCEMENT IDEAS

- Encourage children to complete this project without using outlines to create other unique paintings.
- Supply the children with rolling pins to press the paint onto the paper.
- Talk about what happens when the colors mix together on the paintings.

ACTIVITY 117

Mouse Painting

MATERIALS

- A copy of the book *Mouse Paint* by Ellen Stoll Walsh
- Mice toys for cats
- Paint
- Paper
- Paint shirts

CREATIVE PROCESS

Read the book *Mouse Paint* by Ellen Stoll Walsh to the children. When you are finished, ask the children to go to the art area and put on paint shirts. Direct them to choose two paint colors used in the story: red and blue, red and yellow, or blue and yellow. The children will use a toy mouse to paint with. Put the two colors on a sheet of paper and ask children to use the mouse to move the paint around, creating a mouse picture. Talk about what happens when the paint colors mix. Show the children a color wheel so they can find the two colors they chose and see if the mixed color matches the one they created on their paper.

WHAT ARE CHILDREN LEARNING?

Children are learning what happens when colors become mixed. They are using a new tool to create a picture.

ADAPTATION AND ENHANCEMENT IDEAS

- Children can work in pairs. Each child picks a color and moves the mouse around. Partners see what happens when their mice run into each other or cross paths.
- Encourage children to experiment with toy mice made from different materials—for example, a rubber mouse and a felt or cloth mouse.

ACTIVITY 118

Paint Spinner

MATERIALS

○ Salad spinner

○ Water-based paint

○ Circles made from construction paper

○ Scissors

CREATIVE PROCESS

Children use a spinner and paint to make one-of-a-kind art. Cut out circles that will fit inside the spinner. Ask the children to put a circle in the spinner and add paint drops. They then put the cover on and turn the spinner to see how the paint spreads. If you can find a manual spinner, the children can turn the handle themselves. You can then talk about whether they are turning the handle fast or slow and how the speed affects the artwork.

WHAT ARE CHILDREN LEARNING?

Children are working with a new technique to create a piece of art. They are experimenting to see how the artwork is affected by the process.

ADAPTATION AND ENHANCEMENT IDEAS

- When the circles are dry, hang the art from the ceiling. They will continue to spin with the breezes in the classroom.

- Make a circle collage and ask the children to add their colorful pieces of art.

- Let children draw on their circles before they spin them or add glitter and beads to move around inside the spinner.

ACTIVITY 119

Place It Here

MATERIALS

- Magazines and old greeting cards
- Construction paper
- Scissors
- Glue
- Clear contact paper for lamination

CREATIVE PROCESS

In this activity, children will be making individual placemats to use during snack. Have friends and family save old greeting cards. These are typically made from sturdy cardstock and have fun pictures. Pictures from magazines, toy catalogs, or other sources will work as well. Ask each child to pick a colored piece of construction paper for a placemat. Give them the cards and magazines and let them search for and cut out items to glue on the construction paper. Laminate the mats when the children are finished. If parents want to send photographs to use in the art project, these can be added. Make sure they know that the children may cut the photographs into different shapes to fit their ideas.

WHAT ARE CHILDREN LEARNING?

Children are searching through pictures and making selections that interest them. They are using fine-motor skills to flip pages, cut out pictures, and glue them on paper. They are learning that art can also be useful and practical.

ADAPTATION AND ENHANCEMENT IDEAS

- Working together, children can make a group placemat on which they can place snack items and drink containers for the table. Everyone can look for pictures to include on the group mat.
- The children can make seasonal or holiday placemats.
- Ask children to take turns sanitizing the placemats after snack time and putting them away on a shelf or in a cupboard.

ACTIVITY 120

Sticker Story

MATERIALS

○ Stickers of people or animals

○ Paper

○ Pencil

CREATIVE PROCESS

This lesson will help children put thoughts together and work on forming sentences using a sticker for their main character or theme. Provide a collection of stickers for children to choose from. When they have chosen a sticker, ask them to place it at the top of their paper and then write their stories. Even if they are unable to write letters yet, they can make their own marks to express themselves creatively. While they are drawing and writing, ask them to tell you the story of their sticker. Write the words they provide. Always use every word they say to validate the children's language and thoughts.

WHAT ARE CHILDREN LEARNING?

Children are working on maintaining a topic and putting together sentences to tell a story. They are dictating their thoughts and adding their own drawings and writing.

ADAPTATION AND ENHANCEMENT IDEAS

- Add more pages to the children's stories if they choose to make longer statements and include more ideas.

- Ask open-ended questions to those who have trouble formulating thoughts. Eliminate the questions once they become more skilled at sharing ideas.

ACTIVITY 121

Stringers

MATERIALS

○ Bowls

○ Pieces of construction paper

○ Glue

○ Water

○ Yarn of different colors

○ Crayons or markers

○ Scissors

CREATIVE PROCESS

For this project, children use yarn dipped in glue to make designs on paper.

In small bowls, combine glue with water, creating a fairly diluted mixture. Let the children cut pieces of yarn off the skein they have chosen and dip the yarn into the glue-and-water mixture. Children can draw a picture on a piece of construction paper and add the yarn to it, or they can start with a blank page. When they have their yarn ready, they lay it down on their paper. Let the children use as many and as varied pieces of yarn as they want to. They should practice using words like *long* and *short* when they cut their yarn and name its colors. When the yarn has dried, it will be stiff from the glue. Hang the masterpieces in your room or hallway for everyone to enjoy.

WHAT ARE CHILDREN LEARNING?

Children are using fine-motor skills to cut yarn, hold it, and dip it into the glue mixture. They are making decisions about how they want their pictures to look, what colors and lengths of yarn to use, and how many pieces they want to put on the paper. They are exploring their own creativity.

ADAPTATION AND ENHANCEMENT IDEAS

● Use white yarn and add food coloring to the glue-and-water mixture.

● Suggest to the children that they place the yarn on waxed paper instead of construction paper and peel the paper off when the yarn has dried and the glue has hardened.

● Experiment with different types of yarn to get new textures, or ask children to practice tying knots in the yarn before dipping it in the glue.

Chalk Talk

MATERIALS

○ Sidewalk chalk

○ Squirt bottles filled with water

CREATIVE PROCESS

On a nice day, take the children outside and give them each a piece of sidewalk chalk. Have them draw and color with the chalk. They can trade colors with friends. When their pictures are finished, tell the children to use the squirt bottles to spray water on their drawings. This will darken the colors. Then tell the children to stretch out on the ground and outline their bodies with chalk. They can add features and fill in the details of their clothing. Suggest that they add a favorite object to their drawings.

WHAT ARE CHILDREN LEARNING?

Children are using fine-motor skills to create drawings. They are strengthening their fingers when they squeeze the bottles to spray water, and they are improving their coordination when they aim a stream of water at the lines of their drawing. They are discovering what happens to the chalk when it gets wet.

ADAPTATION AND ENHANCEMENT IDEAS

- Suggest to the children that they use two colors of chalk to color in a space. See if the chalk mixes to create a new color when it gets wet.

- Lead children to a flat vertical surface, like a wall of your building. Ask the children to draw pictures, letters, or shapes on the surface, using the water bottles. Talk about what happens to the lines as the water dries.

ACTIVITY 123

Cut It Out

MATERIALS

- ○ Paper
- ○ Scissors
- ○ Glue, tape, or stapler

USING THE TOOL

Using scissors for cutting is challenging for many children. Practice with cutting is an important skill for children, and teachers need to make it motivating and enjoyable. When you create exciting activities to go with scissors, children will be more willing to participate.

Transitions are good times to introduce scissor skills, because cutting activities can be brief or lengthier and more complex, depending on the time available.

Here are some cutting activities to help children refine their scissor skills:

- Draw a large pig on pink paper. Ask the children cut brown paper ovals ("mud") and glue them to the paper.
- Children can cut out circles. Staple or tape those together to make a long caterpillar.
- Children can cut out leaf shapes to put on a tree poster.
- Draw a large tiger or zebra. Children can cut strips of black paper for the stripes.
- Ask children to cut out round white snowballs. Ask them where they are going to put them in the room. These will create a snowstorm indoors. Work on concepts such as *on, under, in, top,* and *bottom* when they tape up the snowballs.
- Provide fish shapes to cut out. When the children have finished, punch a hole at the top of each fish and place all of them on fishing line.

- Draw an oven. Ask the children to cut out pictures of cakes, cookies, and pies to put in the oven.
- Cover a box with felt. Add eyes and ears, and cut a hole for the mouth. Encourage the children to cut out pictures of different foods to feed the box animal.
- Draw a large outline of a flower. Assign each child a color, and provide them with one-inch strips of construction paper. The children cut off small pieces from the strips and paste them on as petals. This creates a beautiful mosaic pattern when it is completed.

WHAT ARE CHILDREN LEARNING?

Children are using scissors to develop fine-motor skills. They are also learning about different shapes when they cut them out, and they are learning to be patient and cut with care.

ADAPTATION AND ENHANCEMENT IDEAS

- Many varieties of scissors are available for children to use. It is important to consult with occupational therapists to find the correct scissors for some children.
- When children are practicing cutting, encourage them to hold the scissors properly. One trick you can use is to place a small sticker on the children's thumbnails. Their thumbs should be on top and not tipped upside down or to the side. In the thumbs-up position, the sticker will be a visible reminder to the child.
- Many craft stores carry scissors that cut various patterns. These scissors may encourage children who are not excited about cutting practice.

ACTIVITY 124

Rolling Around

MATERIALS

○ Cardboard paper towel and toilet paper tubes

○ Art supplies

USING THE MEDIA

Cardboard tubes are great creative craft media. Put plenty of these in the art center for this activity. Add other craft supplies and see what children will choose to make from them. Children may want to paint the tubes, glue them together, or color them. Give them the freedom to make whatever they imagine, and then talk to them about what they are doing. Ask children to provide names for their creations and tell stories about them. You will be surprised at their creations.

WHAT ARE CHILDREN LEARNING?

Children are building fine-motor skills and finger dexterity along with exploring creative outlets. Through this activity, you will foster creativity, and each child will produce unique results.

ADAPTATION AND ENHANCEMENT IDEAS

● Children can decorate two rolls to make binoculars.

● One tube with beads inside and caps on the ends can turn into a rain stick or maraca for music time.

● Tubes can be glued together as wheels for a car or skis for a snowmobile. A box on the top can house the riders.

● Children can decorate tubes and hook them together for marble races.

● Feature the children's creations on a three-dimensional bulletin board.

● Provide larger mailing tubes as another choice.

ACTIVITY 125
Polar Fluff

MATERIALS

○ Tagboard

○ Glue

○ Shaving cream

○ Bowl

○ Paintbrush

○ Construction paper

○ Decorations, such as wiggle eyes, sequins, fabric pieces

USING THE MEDIA

This project uses glue and shaving cream mixed to create a unique foam. Let children tell you how they want to make use of the foam. They can start with tagboard shapes like snowballs, a polar bear, or a snowman. Pour about a half cup of school glue into a cereal bowl. Add shaving cream to fill up the bowl. Use a paintbrush to mix the two together. Encourage the children to paint the foamy mixture onto their shapes. They can add other items, such as eyes, fabric, sequins, or construction paper shapes. The glue in the mixture will help these items stick. Allow at least a day for the projects to dry, depending on how thick the foam is.

WHAT ARE CHILDREN LEARNING?

Children are exploring creativity and enjoying nice sensory experiences. Encourage children to feel the sticky foam both wet and dry. Talk about the differences in texture.

ADAPTATION AND ENHANCEMENT IDEAS

● Hang these projects in the hall to share with other classes—they are always a favorite. It is difficult for other children to resist touching the projects; they can't help wanting to feel the foam. Put up a sample with a note asking curious friends to keep their hands off the children's projects but to please feel the foam on the sample. The children's work may have to be hung high on the wall to avoid wandering fingers.

● Food coloring can be added to this mixture to create colorful foam. It can be used to make an orange pumpkin, beautiful flowers, or a green tree.

ACTIVITY 126

Dough Fun

MATERIALS

- ○ Homemade cookie dough
- ○ Cocoa or vanilla
- ○ Cookie cutters
- ○ Rolling pins
- ○ Spatulas
- ○ Cookie sheets

USING THE MEDIA

In this activity, children strengthen their hands by manipulating the dough and express themselves by forming structures. Make your favorite dough recipe. Instead of putting all the flour in the recipe, substitute cocoa for half of the flour. This gives your dough a wonderful chocolaty smell and a deep brown color. Vanilla can be added to a different batch for another scent. Let children explore the dough with their hands—folding, mixing, and flattening. Let them use the rolling pins and cookie cutters to make cookie shapes and put them on sheets for baking. Encourage children to use language to talk about what they are making and what they are doing to the dough. They can pound, roll, or squish it between their fingers, or form it into shapes.

NOTE: *Caution children about eating the raw dough.*

WHAT ARE CHILDREN LEARNING?

Children are exploring with all their senses. While they are playing, talk about what they feel, smell, and see.

ADAPTATION AND ENHANCEMENT IDEAS

- Use different spices in the dough.
- Empty frosting tubs and sprinkle containers can be used as children pretend to decorate their cookies after they are done baking.
- Birthday candles can be put in the area so children can make "cakes" and practice their counting skills when they place the candles on top.

Toothbrush Painting

MATERIALS

- ○ Construction paper
- ○ Paint
- ○ Old toothbrushes
- ○ Camera

USING THE TOOL

This is a painting activity using a toothbrush in place of a regular paintbrush. The children can brush back and forth with a toothbrush on construction paper, making lines and shapes and mixing colors. Take photos of the children with big smiles to put with their finished paintings. Either after or before this activity, arrange for a dentist or dental hygienist to visit your classroom. Ask the visitor to talk to the children about the importance of brushing and flossing their teeth. Dentists and hygienists can describe their jobs and answer any questions the children have.

WHAT ARE CHILDREN LEARNING?

Children are learning a valuable life skill. This hands-on activity helps them understand the importance of taking good care of their teeth. At the same time, they are developing the fine-motor skills they need to brush their teeth effectively. The guest speaker reinforces this life skill while talking with the children.

ADAPTATION AND ENHANCEMENT IDEAS

- When people from the dental profession visit a preschool, they often bring toothbrushes for the children. Ask the children to practice brushing their teeth after they have snack. Discuss foods that help their teeth and foods that cause cavities.

- Put up a chart in the classroom, and ask children to put a mark on it if they visit the dentist during the year.

- Make a videotape of yourself at the dentist getting your teeth cleaned.

ACTIVITY 128

Sock Art

MATERIALS

○ Tube socks

○ Sand or very fine gravel

○ Rubber bands

○ Fabric pieces

○ Glue

○ Art supplies

USING THE MEDIA

Ask each child to bring a tube sock to school. The children can help to fill the end of each sock with sand or some other filling. Put a rubber band around the section. Encourage children to decide how many sections they want, and help add filling and rubber bands until they achieve the result they want. They can then decorate their socks using fabrics and other art materials. They may make a snowman, a snake, or a caterpillar. Use the finished projects to talk about differences and creativity with the class. Count the number of sections on the different socks.

WHAT ARE CHILDREN LEARNING?

Children are using their imagination to create a project. They are learning how to discriminate between the concepts of *same* and *different*. They are learning the concepts of *empty* and *full*. They practice counting and talking about ideas like *more* and *less*.

ADAPTATION AND ENHANCEMENT IDEAS

● Hide the completed projects around the room. Ask the children to look for them each day when they arrive. Talk about where the projects are hiding, such as under a table, in a cupboard, or high on a shelf.

● Ask children to write or dictate stories about the adventures of their sock creations.

ACTIVITY 129

Making Tracks

MATERIALS

○ Paint

○ Paint trays

○ Paint shirts

○ A variety of toy cars with rolling wheels

○ Construction paper

USING THE TOOL

In this lesson, children use toy cars to make tracks on paper. Pour paint into paint trays. After the children put on paint shirts, they can drive their cars through the trays of paint and onto construction paper. Tell them to use different colors. Talk about color mixing and see if they can make different colors with their wheels. Also talk about the different tracks and how the wheels look that make the tracks. Some tracks may be wider than others or have different designs. When children are done painting, ask them to pick out their favorite color of construction paper to cut out a frame for their art. Ask children to sign their work. Hang the pictures in the classroom, creating a gallery of tire track art.

WHAT ARE CHILDREN LEARNING?

Children are learning how to mix colors. They are developing fine-motor skills when they move their cars from one area to another. Talk to them about how everyone used the same materials but each piece looks different and unique.

ADAPTATION AND ENHANCEMENT IDEAS

On a nice day, spread a large piece of paper outside. Encourage the children to make a classroom artwork by driving all of their cars on it.

ACTIVITY 130

Painted Fingers

MATERIALS

○ Paint or ink pads

○ Paper

USING THE MEDIA

Children make fingerprints on paper to complete this project. Ask them to place their fingers in paint or on ink pads and then make prints on construction paper. When their fingerprints dry, they can add lines and drawings to them to create different things, such as flowers, animals, or vehicles. Some children may simply wish to make different colored prints and not add to them.

WHAT ARE CHILDREN LEARNING?

Children are using their imaginations to turn their fingerprints into something else by adding more details. They are learning about what happens when colors are mixed with each other.

ADAPTATION AND ENHANCEMENT IDEAS

● Suggest to the children that they make toe prints or even nose prints to see how different these look from fingerprints.

● The children can put one print on a big circle and add their names to it. Make sure you add your print as well. Look at the prints of different fingers and see which ones are bigger or smaller. Be sure students understand that fingerprints are unique; no two people have the same fingerprints.

ACTIVITY 131

Shadow Art

MATERIALS

- ○ Light source
- ○ Marker
- ○ Items to trace
- ○ Paper
- ○ Tape
- ○ Art materials

USING THE TOOL

In this activity, children create a shadow outline. Tape a large piece of paper to the wall. Use a projector or other light source to create an illuminated area on the paper. Ask the children to choose objects to put in front of the light source to cast shadows on the paper. Encourage them to trace around the shadows. They can decorate the outlines with crayons and craft materials. The children can share their creations and see if their classmates can guess what objects they used to produce the shadows.

WHAT ARE CHILDREN LEARNING?

Children are practicing the fine-motor skill of tracing and decorating their artwork. They are choosing objects and guessing what the other children's objects are.

ADAPTATION AND ENHANCEMENT IDEAS

- Ask the children to stand in front of the light source and trace their profiles. Encourage them to decorate their own outlines. Display these and see if their friends can identify their profiles. Share these at conference time with parents.

- Use the shadow outlines during circle time to play a guessing game. Hold up each outline and see if the children can find the object that matches. Maybe they will remember who decorated the shadow.

ACTIVITY 132

Light as a Feather

MATERIALS

○ Construction paper bird shapes

○ Feathers

○ Paint

○ Glue

USING THE TOOL

Children will make a bird using feathers in different ways. Tell children to choose a construction paper bird in the color of their choice. Then ask them to use feathers to paint the bird or glue the feathers on their bird. Then hang the birds in the window or from the ceiling.

WHAT ARE CHILDREN LEARNING?

Children are using feathers as unconventional art tools. Doing so helps spark their imaginations and encourages them to look for other items that can be used for other projects.

ADAPTATION AND ENHANCEMENT IDEAS

● Add bird books to the classroom so children can page through and find birds that are exciting or interesting to them.

● Put binoculars at the window so children can look out for birds flying in the sky or nesting in trees. Put a bird feeder outside the classroom window to attract different birds to your area.

ACTIVITY 133

Something's Afoot

MATERIALS

○ Large sheets of paper

○ Tape

○ Paints

○ Paintbrushes

○ Warm, soapy water

○ Towels

USING THE TOOL

Children will use their feet to paint in this project. Place large sheets of paper on an uncarpeted floor. Tape the pieces down so they don't move. Allow children to choose paint colors and then paint the bottoms of their feet with a paintbrush. Talk about how the paint feels as it is brushed on the different parts of the foot like the toes, heel, and sole. Let children walk around on the paper, creating colored footprints. They can tiptoe, slide, or stomp to see how the prints change. Talk about what happens when their colors mix with those of their friends. Following the activity, wash the children's feet in warm, soapy water.

WHAT ARE CHILDREN LEARNING?

Children are learning how to balance while moving with the slippery paint on their feet. They are experimenting with paint and colors and watching them mix while they walk around. They are learning about body parts and sensations like *cold* and *slippery*. Talk about what the water feels like when it cleans off their feet.

ADAPTATION AND ENHANCEMENT IDEAS

● This activity can occur outside on a nice day, and you can use a garden hose to wash off the children's feet.

● Paint the bottoms of old shoes to see what types of tracks they make on the paper. Children can put either their feet or their hands into the shoes to make the prints.

ACTIVITY 134

Marble Paintings

MATERIALS

○ Paper

○ Marbles

○ Paint

○ Shirt boxes

○ Paint shirts

USING THE TOOL

In this activity, children are exploring how to use marbles as painting tools. If you have a theme for the week, cut out related outlines for the children, such as hearts or trees. This project is just as fun when you use a whole sheet of paper and allow the children to cut out their own shapes after the painted paper is dry. Place the paper, marbles, and blobs of the child's choice of paint colors in a shirt box. Ask children to hold the edges of the box and tip them back and forth to roll the marbles around, making paint trails. Frame the pictures, or ask the children to cut out designs when the paper is dry.

WHAT ARE CHILDREN LEARNING?

Children are using their motor skills to shake the box and move the marbles. They are creating unique pieces of art. When they choose the paints to use, they can work on color names.

ADAPTATION AND ENHANCEMENT IDEAS

- The children can use marbles of different sizes to see if it is easier or more difficult to move them around in the box.

- Ask the children to think of other things to put into the box for painting, and let them try out their ideas.

- Use a tube that can be closed at both ends, such as a potato chip tube. Add paper, paint, and marbles, and encourage the children to shake the tube to make artwork.

ACTIVITY 135

Rubbings

MATERIALS

○ Paper

○ Tape

○ Leaves

○ Crayons

USING THE MEDIA

For this activity, the children will explore nature and use the leaves that they collect to create a project. Tell them to go outside to search for fallen leaves. Ask them to bring the leaves back inside and arrange them on a flat table. Place a piece of paper over the top of the arrangement and tape it down at the corners. Provide the children with crayons, and ask them to draw back and forth over the leaves. Doing so will create a rubbing of the leaves on the paper. Hang their leaf prints up when they are done.

WHAT ARE CHILDREN LEARNING?

Children are bringing nature indoors. They are using their fine-motor skills to create the rubbings from the leaves. They are observing textures and patterns while they work.

ADAPTATION AND ENHANCEMENT IDEAS

- Ask children to look for other items they can use for rubbings.

- Let the children experiment with thickness to discover which items work well and which items are more difficult.

- Children can experiment with chalk, colored pencils, and other media to see which work best for rubbings.

ACTIVITY 136

Glue Designs

MATERIALS

○ Glue

○ Food coloring

○ Construction paper of several colors

○ Markers

USING THE MEDIA

Prior to the activity, add food coloring to bottles of glue. Give children the glue bottles, and let them pick out the colored paper they want. Have them squeeze the glue from the bottles to make lines and drawings on their paper. Let the glue dry overnight, and then see if the children want to color in their line drawings. Introduce words such as *wet* and *sticky* while they are working, and discuss how the glue changes when it is dry. Encourage them to touch the dried lines and talk about how they feel.

WHAT ARE CHILDREN LEARNING?

Children are using a common art medium, glue, in a different way. Many children glue items, but they don't really see how the glue changes when it dries, since it is typically hidden under paper. When they squeeze the bottles, the children are using the muscles in their hands and developing motor skills.

ADAPTATION AND ENHANCEMENT IDEAS

- Add buttons, sequins, or other materials so children can add these to their glue creations. They may especially enjoy adding glitter to the glue while it is still wet.

- Ask children to write their names with the glue.

ACTIVITY 137

Bubble Up

MATERIALS

○ Paints

○ Paintbrushes

○ Bubble wrap

○ Construction paper

USING THE MEDIA

Give each child a piece of bubble wrap. Have the children paint over the bubbles with their paintbrushes. Then give them construction paper to lay over the bubbles. Ask them to gently press down to transfer the paint from the bubbles to the paper. Then help them peel the paper away from the bubbles. Let the art dry overnight.

WHAT ARE CHILDREN LEARNING?

Children are experimenting with bubble wrap and paints. They are discovering how paint can be transferred from one surface to another. They are experimenting with colors and color mixing.

ADAPTATION AND ENHANCEMENT IDEAS

- Children can cut shapes from the bubble wrap before painting it. They can dip one large bubble in paint and use it to make prints.

- Children can cut out designs from bubble wrap and glue them on paper.

- Encourage children to pop the bubbles. To do so, they need to use their muscles by squeezing their fingers together.

- Give the children fingerpaints, and let them rub the paints onto the bubbles with their hands.

ACTIVITY 138

Magnetic Pull

MATERIALS

○ Paper plates

○ Paint

○ Magnetic animals

○ Strong magnets

USING THE TOOL

During this activity, children discover how magnets attract when they use them to create paintings. Experiment before the activity with your magnets so you know they will easily move the animal pieces. Ask children to work in pairs, and give each pair a paper plate. Have them squirt paint on it. Then children place a magnetized animal on the plate. While one child holds the plate, the other moves a strong magnet underneath, causing the animal to move around, spreading the paint. Give the pairs a second plate and ask them to trade places so the other child can have a turn.

WHAT ARE CHILDREN LEARNING?

Children are learning how magnets attract. They are working together with partners and taking turns during the project.

ADAPTATION AND ENHANCEMENT IDEAS

Children can glue their animal onto the plate if they want it as part of their artwork when they are done moving it around.

ACTIVITY 139

Rip It Up

MATERIALS

○ Books and magazines

○ Construction paper

○ Permanent marker

○ Glue

USING THE MEDIA

Tearing paper is an effective way for children to strengthen their hands and fingers. Ask them what they want to make. Place books or magazines in the art center for them to look through if they need a little help getting inspired. Draw an outline of the object they choose. You can also give them an outline that focuses on a theme, such as a flower or an animal. Give the children pieces of construction paper and ask them to rip up small pieces and glue them onto their outlines. They can use glue bottles or glue sticks, or you can fill small cups with glue for the children to dip pieces into the glue. They can use any colors they choose and make their pieces large or small.

WHAT ARE CHILDREN LEARNING?

Children are choosing an item they want to make. They are strengthening their fingers by tearing the paper pieces. They are making creative decisions about colors of paper and where to glue them. Learning how to tear paper helps them when they need to tear off paper towels for drying their hands.

ADAPTATION AND ENHANCEMENT IDEAS

● Ask children to tear paper to make leaves or apples on a tree.

● Children can choose colors and make their own sections of a rainbow for a group project.

ACTIVITY 140

Foam Art

MATERIALS

○ Different shapes and sizes of foam objects
○ Art materials
○ Toothpicks

USING THE MEDIA

Include foam circles, packaging pieces, and other shapes in the art center. Add paints, glue, and other supplies for building things from the objects or decorating. Ask the children to feel the foam and discover what it sounds like when they brush their fingers across it. The foam pieces can be painted, glued, stuck together with toothpicks, or used like paintbrushes or stamps to create artwork on paper.

WHAT ARE CHILDREN LEARNING?

Children are making art projects in a medium with fun textures to explore.

ADAPTATION AND ENHANCEMENT IDEAS

- Save different types of packaging materials and use them as stamps with paint or ink.

- Add packaging materials to the water table for a tactile experience. See if the materials float or sink in the water.

CHAPTER 5

Learning Games

Games teach children how to take turns, cooperate, and work toward goals. In the right environment, games promote good sportsmanship and positive competition. In this chapter, you will find original ideas for games grouped into four categories: board games, thinking games, verbal games, and movement games. When you use the games, notice how helpful they can be in refocusing the children's energy and making them more alert for learning.

BOARD GAMES

Playing board games is a great way to reinforce turn-taking skills and cooperation. Many commercial games focus on pre-academic skills. Sometimes, however, teachers need games to match specific skills or themes. You can make your own game boards by starting with existing board games and remaking them to suit your needs. Use old boards and add your own pictures to match your objectives. Add stickers to your game boards of popular characters to create interest. Use an old deck of cards with new pictures of your choice glued on. Add dice, spinners, and space markers.

You can also start from scratch. Many of the board game ideas that follow explain how to make them from common classroom materials. You can usually make game boards from tagboard in shapes to match your theme or unit. Make your own dice from blocks. If you only want smaller numbers, you can write only 1s and 2s on each side. Alternatively, color each side of the block if you prefer children to move their game pieces to a color. Or paint wooden shapes different colors, put them in a small bag, and tell the child to pull out a shape and move to the next color or shape that matches on the game board.

THINKING GAMES

The games in this section help to build thinking skills. For example, some games require children to rely on memory or to categorize to progress. Skills like matching, sequencing, predicting, counting, and recognizing relationships between objects come wrapped here in fun and games.

VERBAL GAMES

These games are designed to get children listening and speaking. Whether the games feature rhymes or require daily conversational skills, they encourage language development.

MOVEMENT GAMES

These games help to develop all types of motor skills. Use the games to get children up and moving, and notice the energy shift that results. Whether children have too much energy or seem sluggish, these games provide a way to help them refocus.

ACTIVITY 141

Lights Out

MATERIALS

○ Flashlight

○ Game board with pictures on each space

○ Copies of the pictures used on the game board

GAME SETUP

In this game, children use a flashlight to find certain spaces on a game board. Create a board that features pictures of things that your class is working on: for example, colors, shapes, animals, numbers, or objects whose names begin with a specific sound. Put one picture on each square of the board. Designate one square as the starting point by writing *START* or using a symbol like a green light. Make sure the squares are large enough so the flashlight can focus on a single square. Use the copies of all the pictures as the deck. Dim the lights.

HOW TO PLAY

Have the children take turns drawing a card. The child with the turn shines the flashlight on the starting point, and then moves the light along the game board path, stopping on the square that matches the card. Spend some time talking about the item before the next child's turn. Children will want second turns, so be sure to allow enough time for them.

WHAT ARE CHILDREN LEARNING?

Children are learning matching skills and working on academic vocabulary. Following the path with the flashlight helps them work on fine-motor control.

ADAPTATION AND ENHANCEMENT IDEAS

● Hanging your game board on the wall works well because everyone can watch the path of the light.

● You can create a board featuring photographs of the children in your class. The children can choose a picture of a classmate and look for that person on the board. Ask them to share something they like about that friend.

ACTIVITY 142

Sounds Like a Bingo

MATERIALS

○ Pictures

○ Tagboard

○ Pennies or other space holders

○ CD or MP3 player and recorded environmental sounds

○ Prizes, such as stickers or treats

GAME SETUP

This is a bingo game using sounds. Make a CD or MP3 recording of environmental sounds. Leave a pause between each sound. Find pictures or photos that match the sounds. Make bingo boards with the pictures on them. Use the *B-I-N-G-O* letters across the top, or use colors or shapes if the children don't know their letters yet. Talk to them about filling in a row or column and shouting "Bingo!" or another fun phrase. Play the game blackout style if it is difficult for your class to understand the rows and columns.

HOW TO PLAY

Play the CD and ask children to listen for the sound that matches each picture. They use pennies or other space holders to cover the correct picture when they hear the matching sound. Keep going until everyone has filled in a row or column. You may need to play a sound more than once so all the children can identify it.

WHAT ARE CHILDREN LEARNING?

Children are learning how to listen carefully and match a sound with a picture. This sound-to-source matching is a key skill in building phonemic awareness. The children also are learning the rules of a popular game they will probably play many times in their school years.

ADAPTATION AND ENHANCEMENT IDEAS

- This game concept can be used with almost any theme. Play farm or zoo bingo with animal sounds and pictures. You can record different teachers' voices and see if the children can match their photos to their voices.

- Make a conceptual bingo in which the children look at pictures depicting positional words spoken on the CD, including *over*, *under*, *in the middle*, and *behind*.

- A social bingo game uses pictures that show people laughing, crying, screaming, and so on—with the emotions named on the CD.

- Social scenarios can be depicted in pictures, such as a child helping another or two children waving good-bye to each other. The CD offers language matching, such as, "Can I help you?" or "Bye, I'll see you later."

ACTIVITY 143

Dress the Snowman

MATERIALS

- ○ Tagboard
- ○ Construction paper
- ○ Velcro
- ○ Brad fastener

GAME SETUP

Make several tagboard game boards with the outline of a snowman. For every snowman, make construction paper pieces of six items: face, hat, scarf, broom, mittens, and boots. Add Velcro strips to the pieces and tagboard so the pieces can be attached to the game boards. Using tagboard and a brad fastener, make a spinner that features the same six items.

HOW TO PLAY

Each child chooses a game board. They take turns spinning the wheel. When they land on an item, they find the matching piece and place it in the correct spot on their snowman board. The winner is the child that completes a snowman most quickly.

WHAT ARE CHILDREN LEARNING?

Children are learning to take turns and to match when they find all the items for the snowman.

ADAPTATION AND ENHANCEMENT IDEAS

- Depending on the children's attention level, you can add additional spaces on the spinner. A space indicating "choose anything" can be used to increase the chance of landing on a needed item.
- Instead of spinners, dice can be used with pictures of the items on the sides.

ACTIVITY 144

Train Car Categories

MATERIALS

- ○ Tagboard
- ○ Markers
- ○ Pictures
- ○ Game pieces
- ○ Dice
- ○ Poker chips

GAME SETUP

Make a board with spaces in a circle. On each space, place a picture that matches one of four categories: vehicles, food, clothing, and animals. Make enough game cards for the number of children who will participate. Each card features a picture of a train with four cars. Each train car pictures something that belongs to one of the four categories.

HOW TO PLAY

Children place their game piece on any space on the board to start. Have the first child shake the dice, move her piece the correct number of spaces, identify the picture, and name the category in which the object belongs. The child then places a chip on the correct car on the train card. The winner is the child who fills the train card first by landing on one item from each category.

WHAT ARE CHILDREN LEARNING?

Children are learning how to categorize items. For example, if they land on a cow or tiger, they match it to the animal on their train car. An apple or hamburger is matched to the food car. Children are learning counting skills by moving their game piece forward the number of dots on the die.

ADAPTATION AND ENHANCEMENT IDEAS

- Use more challenging categories for more advanced students. Use instruments, hot things, or items that fly, for example.
- Focus the categories on colors or emotions.

ACTIVITY 145

Shape Spinner

MATERIALS

○ Construction paper

○ Tagboard

○ Brad fasteners

○ Pictures or photographs

GAME SETUP

Shape Spinner focuses on matching an item to its graphic representation. Make a square game board with four sections, and place an outline of a different shape in each section. Make an arrow from tagboard and use a brad fastener to attach it to your board. Find pictures or take photographs of items shaped like them on your board—for example, a cookie, wheel, and ball for circles; a sailboat, piece of pie, and pennant for triangles; a block, window, and picture frame for squares; and a door, domino, and book for rectangles. The number of pictures determines how long the game will last.

HOW TO PLAY

Ask children to take turns spinning the arrow. They should name the shape they land on and then find a picture that matches that shape. They take turns until all of the pictures have been used.

WHAT ARE CHILDREN LEARNING?

Children are focusing on shape recognition. They are matching symbols to items with the same shape. They are learning and using new vocabulary words.

ADAPTATION AND ENHANCEMENT IDEAS

- Use more shapes on your game board to increase the children's vocabulary and to challenge them.

- Instead of asking them to match, tell the children look to around the classroom and find items with the shapes they have spun. Children may also think of items that are not in the classroom, such as wheels on a car or a triangular roof.

- The game board can also use colors, written numerals (match to pictures with the same number of items), letters (match to pictures of items that start with that sound), or feelings (facial expressions match to scenes that go along with the emotions).

ACTIVITY 146

Who, What, Where

MATERIALS

○ Tagboard
○ Stickers
○ Bag
○ Painted wooden pieces
○ Space holders

GAME SETUP

Many children need practice thinking about and answering questions. Make a board from tagboard to help them with these challenges. The game squares should have different colors. Every few squares, place a sticker. Make a collection of cards, each with a question written on it. The questions should focus on children's responses to situations, such as "How would you feel if a friend did not want to play with you?" or "What would you do if you saw a friend fall down?" Paint wooden game pieces different colors to match the colors on the squares. Place the game pieces in a bag.

HOW TO PLAY

When the game starts, the first player reaches into the bag, pulls out a painted piece, and moves the space holder to that color. If the child lands on a spot with a sticker, she draws a card and hands it to you to read the question. Listen to her answer and prompt her if more information is needed. After each turn, the child returns the colored piece to the bag and shakes it up for the next player. Children move along the board until someone gets to the end of the path.

WHAT ARE CHILDREN LEARNING?

Children are matching colors, taking turns, comprehending questions, and giving verbal answers. They are practicing social responses to situations when they think about how they would act.

ADAPTATION AND ENHANCEMENT IDEAS

- Think of questions that will challenge and expand children's verbal and social skills. Add more challenging questions for those who have good verbal and comprehension skills.

- Use personal information, such as birth dates, phone numbers, and addresses.

- Use picture cards and ask questions about what is happening in the photos.

ACTIVITY 147

Hands-On Bingo

MATERIALS

○ Camera

○ Picture boards

○ Items to match each picture

○ Bag

○ Space holders

GAME SETUP

This is a bingo board game that uses real objects instead of pictures. Find several small items to use for your bingo game and take pictures of them. Copy the pictures and make several bingo boards with the pictures so children can play together. Place the items in a bag.

HOW TO PLAY

The first child should reach into the bag to pull out an item. All players find the space on their boards that matches the item and cover it with a space holder. Then the player returns the item to the bag so another child can pull out an item. Children continue pulling out items until someone has a row or column filled.

WHAT ARE CHILDREN LEARNING?

Children are matching items to pictures. They are thinking about what they need to find to win and using their sense of touch to try to find that item when they pull items from the bag.

ADAPTATION AND ENHANCEMENT IDEAS

- Items can be from your weekly theme of a particular shape or of a category (for example, animals).

- Create a board with seasonal items, and children can pull out a mitten or sunglasses and talk about the season that item is used in.

ACTIVITY 148

Parts of the Whole

MATERIALS

- ○ Tagboard
- ○ Pictures of parts of items
- ○ Matching whole items that go along with the parts
- ○ Space holders
- ○ Colored squares
- ○ Dice

GAME SETUP

The objective of this board game is to have children think about how parts of an object relate to the whole object. Make a game board with square spaces, including one labeled *START.* Display the collection of items close to the game area. Place a picture of a part of an item every few squares on the board—for example, a wheel, a cat's tail, or a fish's fin.

HOW TO PLAY

Children begin on *START*, roll the dice, and move to their spaces. When they land on a space with a part, they look at the collection of items and find the whole that matches the part. They keep this item, cover up the space with a colored square, and leave their space holder there until the next turn. Other players must skip the marked squares. The game continues until all the players reach the end of the board. They can count the number of items they have collected to see who has the most.

WHAT ARE CHILDREN LEARNING?

Children are learning about part-to-whole relationships. They are counting spaces and items they have collected.

💡 ADAPTATION AND ENHANCEMENT IDEAS

- Ask children to talk about each item they collect—what it does, how it feels, or where it can be found. See if they can name other parts of the objects, such as fur on the cat or the steering wheel on the car.

- Allow children to play with and explore the items from the collection after the game is done. See what kinds of connections they make with the objects.

ACTIVITY 149

Weather Expressions

MATERIALS

○ Tagboard

○ Weather pictures

○ Space holders

○ Spinner with sections for each color on the game board

○ Rainbow stickers

GAME SETUP

This board game spurs children to think about seasons and weather. Make a board with colored spaces, a space labeled *START,* and a spinner with color sections corresponding to the spaces on the board. Every three spaces on the board, place a picture depicting weather, such as rain, snow, sunshine, and wind.

HOW TO PLAY

Children begin at *START*, spin the spinner, and move to the first square of that color. Every time players land on a weather space, ask them to describe something they could do in that type of weather. Talk about clothing they would wear or activities they could do outside. After they give their answers, offer them a rainbow sticker. When every player gets to the end of the board, see how many stickers each child has collected.

WHAT ARE CHILDREN LEARNING?

Children are using the concepts of color and weather when they move along the board. They are using expressive language to talk about what they could do in different kinds of weather.

ADAPTATION AND ENHANCEMENT IDEAS

● Use the stickers children collect to make a rainbow poster—it will brighten up the classroom.

● Ask the children to look outside and then decide which pictures match the weather.

● While they are playing the game, talk to the children about seasons. Ask them which pictures match summer or winter. If they are learning the months, ask them to name the months in which they see snow or hot, sunny days.

ACTIVITY 150

Concepts Cards

MATERIALS

- ○ Tagboard (red and blue)
- ○ Pictures
- ○ Items, such as a ball, toy cat, book, shoe, and pillow
- ○ Large bag
- ○ Table

GAME SETUP

This is a card game that requires children to follow directions and develop positional concepts and awareness of body parts. Make two sets of picture cards from tagboard: one set is red and illustrates positional concepts such as *in*, *under*, *over*, *around*, *beside*, and *behind*. The other set is blue and illustrates body parts like *head*, *foot*, *hand*, *arm*, *leg*, *back*, and *ear*. Use a table to hold the props and cards; children can move around it when following the directions. Put the items you have chosen into the bag.

HOW TO PLAY

Ask a child to pick an item from the bag and then turn over the top card in each set of cards. Point to the cards while you make up directions based on them. For example, if the child picks a toy cat out of the bag and turns

cards over with the words *under* and *head*, you can give a direction like "Put the cat on your head and crawl under the table." See if the child can remember and follow your directions. (This game may require an additional adult to help with the directions and keep the game moving along.)

WHAT ARE CHILDREN LEARNING?

Children are practicing memory skills when they follow your spoken directions. They are also building vocabulary about positions and body parts. As they move their bodies, they are working on motor skills.

⚙ ADAPTATION AND ENHANCEMENT IDEAS

- If you need the game to be more challenging, add another set of cards. Alternatively, instead of using only the table, include other items from the classroom as stationary objects. This will be one more thing the children have to remember.

- Store items from your story for the day in the bag for children to choose from. This will reinforce your classroom theme.

- Label the cards with a position or body part word.

ACTIVITY 151

Make a Match

MATERIALS

○ File folders

○ Matching pairs of images

○ Glue

○ Plastic storage bags

○ Large rubber bands

GAME SETUP

Many teachers use folder games to help children learn matching skills. Purchase boxes of Valentine cards on sale after the holiday. Most Valentine boxes come with several sets of the same cards, so your matches are already there. The cards usually feature favorite characters. This makes the games motivating for children. Glue one card to a folder and save another for its match. If you can, laminate your folders and cards so they will last longer. To store the game, place the loose cards in a bag and wrap a rubber band (or two) around the bag and folders.

HOW TO PLAY

Partners or individuals can enjoy making matches. To play the game, a child chooses a picture card from the bag and places it in the corresponding folder.

WHAT ARE CHILDREN LEARNING?

Children are practicing matching skills when they put like items together. They are also using vocabulary to talk about the characters and other pictures they see.

ADAPTATION AND ENHANCEMENT IDEAS

- This game can be completed as a turn-taking game with groups or the entire class.

- Save greeting cards to make puzzle games that the children must fit together. Cut the cards in two, glue one piece on the folder, and use the other piece for the match.

- Old wallpaper books can be made into colorful folder games as well. Cut fun shapes out of the patterns for use as matching games.

- Another fun way to play matching games is to use an old coffee can. Cover it with opaque contact paper, and draw shapes on the can with a permanent marker. Make matching shapes, each with a magnet on the back. Children enjoy turning the can around, looking for the same shape, and sticking the magnet to it. Store your pieces inside the cans.

ACTIVITY 152

Flip It Open

MATERIALS

○ File folders

○ Brightly colored pictures

○ Velcro

GAME SETUP

Cut several one- or two-inch windows in the front of a file folder. For each window, cut three sides of a square, creating a flap that opens and closes. Place a piece of Velcro on the outside of each window to hold it open. Put pictures of colors, shapes, animals, or numbers on the windows so children can name them. Now place a page-sized picture inside the folder. Find pictures that will elicit language and encourage emotional responses. Look through toy catalogs or old calendars for such images.

HOW TO PLAY

The children take turns telling you which window to open. For example, a child may ask you to open the orange window. Each time you open a window, it reveals part of the picture in the folder. Ask the children to guess what the picture will look like. When all the windows have been opened, show them the picture inside. Tell them to pat themselves on the back if they guess correctly. Children can share their feelings about the pictures and talk about what they would do in the picture scenarios.

WHAT ARE CHILDREN LEARNING?

Children are discovering how a part relates to the whole. They are learning vocabulary and discovering how to build on information from their peers. Often, children will offer responses that do not match the picture they see. They quickly learn how to listen to others' ideas and to choose one that makes more sense. Be sure to accept all ideas and then allow children to discover what is inside together.

ADAPTATION AND ENHANCEMENT IDEAS

- This is a quick game to pull out if you have a few minutes during a transition, when you are waiting for children to come together after another project, or at the end of the day.

- Offer pictures of different facial expressions. Cut the holes in the folders strategically so the eyes, nose, and mouth are revealed when the windows are opened. Ask children to share why they think the eyes look sad or the mouth looks happy.

ACTIVITY 153

Bottled Up

MATERIALS

○ Empty, clean soda pop bottles (different sizes)

○ Marbles, sand, pebbles, water, or other media to fill the bottles

○ Small objects that fit inside the bottles

GAME SETUP

Fill each bottle with a different material. Then add a small object to some of the bottles. Glue or tape the tops of the bottles to prevent spills.

HOW TO PLAY

Children turn and spin the bottles to discover what is inside—for example, a bottle with pebbles may also contain small plastic animals. A bottle with water may hold white glitter that looks like snow when it's shaken. Bottles with soft pom-poms or loud bells can be used to compare sound volume.

WHAT ARE CHILDREN LEARNING?

Children are exploring the bottles and the different items inside. They shake, tip, and roll the bottles to see what happens to the materials. Different-sized bottles can help children learn about sizes and weight.

ADAPTATION AND ENHANCEMENT IDEAS

● Put the bottles in the water table or a large container as a discovery center.

● Make accompanying cards with pictures of the objects that are inside for some bottles. See if the children can move the bottles so all the items on the picture card are revealed.

● Let the children help find items to go inside the bottles. See if they can problem solve if the items they choose are too big.

ACTIVITY 154

What's Missing, Snowman?

MATERIALS

○ Felt
○ Felt board

GAME SETUP

Cut felt pieces into three large circles to represent a snowman. Add colorful felt pieces for a hat, scarf, eyes, nose, mouth, boots, arms, mittens, and buttons. Assemble the snowman on a felt board so the children can see all the pieces displayed.

HOW TO PLAY

The children take turns in this activity, closing their eyes while you remove one piece of the snowman. One by one, they take turns opening their eyes and trying to remember which item is missing.

WHAT ARE CHILDREN LEARNING?

Children are using observation and memory to identify what is missing. They are matching items and identifying body parts and clothing. They are learning to wait for their turn and to encourage their classmates.

ADAPTATION AND ENHANCEMENT IDEAS

- To challenge some children, you can take away more than one item at a time.
- Pictures of each item can be available as a hint for children who cannot identify the items that are missing.
- Ask the children to pretend to be the teacher and take items away for their friends.
- Make two snowmen. As you remove items from one snowman or the other, ask children how the snowmen are different.
- Photograph the snowman with some but not all of the items, and see if the children can recreate him on the felt board with the items in the picture.

ACTIVITY 155

Package Clues

MATERIALS

○ A decorated box

○ Items with specific textures to place in the box

○ Pictures

○ Tagboard

GAME SETUP

Decorate a box with wrapping paper, stickers, or construction paper. Select different items to place inside it. Make a tagboard card for each item that provides visual clues about what it is. For example, place a pair of socks in the box. Make a card with pictures depicting clothing and feet.

HOW TO PLAY

Show the clue cards one at a time, and ask the children to guess about each clue. See if they can figure out how all the clues are related and identify the item in the box. When the children have finished guessing and the item is revealed, give them the opportunity to hold and feel the item. Talk about its texture and what the item is used for.

WHAT ARE CHILDREN LEARNING?

Children are learning how to combine and synthesize information. They are thinking about how the pictures can represent a bigger item. They are learning words for textures and colors as they feel and describe the items.

ADAPTATION AND ENHANCEMENT IDEAS

- Make clue cards for items that are connected to your theme for the week.

- Use this activity to introduce a story you will be reading to the children. Ask them to guess the topic of the story based on the items they discover in the box.

- Children can bring items from home to place in the box. Help them provide their own clues to the class.

ACTIVITY 156

Shoe Box Match

MATERIALS

○ Empty shoe boxes, one per child

○ Large bag

GAME SETUP

Hand each child a shoe box. The children sit in a circle on the floor and take their shoes off. Ask them to place one shoe in their box and one shoe in the bag. Stack the boxes with shoes in an area that will be the shoe store during the game.

HOW TO PLAY

Encourage the children to search through the bag to find their own shoe. Once they have found it, they go to the shoe store. There, they can take turns being the store clerk. The clerk must search through the boxes to find the matching shoe. Then the clerk presents the pair and helps the shopper put them on. The customer then takes a turn being the clerk.

WHAT ARE CHILDREN LEARNING?

Children are practicing matching skills and remembering which boxes hold the different shoes. They are working on taking off and putting on shoes, a dressing skill they need every day. They are role-playing a store cashier.

ADAPTATION AND ENHANCEMENT IDEAS

● Add toy money so customers can buy their shoes at the store and the clerk can put the money in the cash register. Add bags so the clerk can package shoe boxes to send home with the customers.

● If the children need further challenges, you can provide related items, such as a sock and a shoe, instead of direct matches. This store game can be played with gloves or mittens and related items like scarves and hats.

ACTIVITY 157

Petal Counters

MATERIALS

- ○ Construction paper
- ○ Scissors
- ○ Markers
- ○ Glue

GAME SETUP

Make ten flowers with long stems from construction paper. Put one petal on the first flower, two on the second, and so on until you have ten flowers. Write the correct number of petals on the back of each flower. Draw ten flowerpots. Cut a narrow hole in each flowerpot so the children can plant a flower stem inside. Write numbers from one to ten on the flowerpots.

HOW TO PLAY

The children choose a flower, count the petals on it, and find the matching pot to plant it in. Allow children to self-correct while they match the numerals on the flowers and pots.

WHAT ARE CHILDREN LEARNING?

Children are learning numbers and using counting skills. They are using fine-motor skills to plant the flowers in the pots.

ADAPTATION AND ENHANCEMENT IDEAS

- This activity can be done independently at a center or by a group.
- Add colored dots on the back of each flower and its corresponding pot to help children who don't know their numerals yet to self-correct. For example, the flower with two petals and the flowerpot with the number *two* will have the same number of colored dots on the back.
- If children need a bigger challenge, add more petals to each flower.
- Make flowers and pots that are the same color and tell children to plant flowers by matching the colors. Make pots with shapes that match the shapes you draw in the centers of the flowers. Use letters on the flowerpot and pictures of things with names that start with the same letters on the flowers.

ACTIVITY 158

Strike One

MATERIALS

○ Felt or construction paper

○ Baseball hats

○ Baseball gloves

GAME SETUP

This game is a version of Memory using real objects instead of cards. Hold a baseball game day. Invite children to wear their favorite baseball hats and jerseys. Make matching pairs of paper baseballs and gloves in different colors. Hide the paper balls under the real baseball hats and the paper gloves under the real baseball gloves. This game can be played by one child or by groups of children.

HOW TO PLAY

Children take turns turning over a hat and a glove to see if they can find a match. When a match is found, leave the hat and glove turned over or remove them from the area. Children keep taking turns until every ball and glove match has been matched. Return the pieces to the game and play again.

WHAT ARE CHILDREN LEARNING?

Children are using memory skills to find the matches. They are also having fun dressing up and sharing their excitement about their favorite baseball teams.

ADAPTATION AND ENHANCEMENT IDEAS

● Put patterns or shapes on the gloves to make the game more challenging.

● Hold a dress-up day for other favorite sports. Make matches for these sports and use them to play the game.

● Watch a clip of a real baseball game on television. If your local school district has a baseball team, see if you can find a video of them playing ball. Then go outside and play catch with soft baseballs and gloves.

Who Took the Honey from the Teddy Bear?

MATERIALS

- ○ Your favorite teddy bear
- ○ A picture of a honey pot
- ○ Enough boxes or containers for each child

GAME SETUP

Children love playing Who Took the Cookie from the Cookie Jar? However, when they try to hide the cookie behind their backs, they often find it difficult to keep their secret. This activity is a variation that alleviates the problem. Hide the honey pot picture in one of the boxes. Then tell the children to form a circle and place a box in front of each child. Tell the children that they can't peek in their boxes. Place your teddy bear in the middle of the circle.

HOW TO PLAY

Teach the following rhyming sequence to the children:

   "[*Child's name*] took the honey from the teddy bear."
   "Who, me?"
   "Yes, you!"
   "It couldn't be!"
   "Then who?"

Choose a child to go first. Ask the class to begin the song using this child's name, and then the child and the class sing it responsively all the way through. Urge the child to open her box to see if she has the honey pot. If so, she should use the honey pot to feed the bear. If not, she names the next classmate, and everyone sings the song again.

WHAT ARE CHILDREN LEARNING?

Children are practicing the names of their friends and learning to wait patiently for a turn to open their boxes. They are using their memory to repeat the song.

 ADAPTATION AND ENHANCEMENT IDEAS

You can play many other variations, including "Who Took the Bone from the Puppy Dog?" or "Who Took the Acorn from the Little Squirrel?" This will become a game that children love to play over and over.

ACTIVITY 160

Drive-Through Window

MATERIALS

- ○ Plastic eggs of many colors, each with a surprise or treat inside
- ○ Basket
- ○ Cardboard
- ○ Stickers or pictures of spring items

GAME SETUP

Decorate the piece of cardboard with bright colors and images of eggs, bunnies, chicks, flowers, and other spring objects. Cut a hole in the middle of the board. Attach the board to a shelf or cabinet so you can see through the hole from both sides. Teach the children the following rhyme, sung to the tune of "The Farmer in the Dell."

[*Name*] wants a blue.

[*Name*] wants a blue.

Heigh ho, did you know,

[*He/She*] wants a blue?

HOW TO PLAY

Choose one child to be the worker who goes behind the decorated board with a basket of colored eggs. The customers sit on the other side of the board. One at a time, they approach the window and tell the worker what color egg they want. The whole class sings the rhyme while the worker searches through the basket for the correct egg. The worker hands the correct egg through the hole. The customer then opens the egg to find the surprise inside. If the customer gets the wrong color, the egg is sent back and the worker tries again. Continue until everyone has a turn being the worker and the customer. After children understand how the game works, they can play on their own during free play or center times.

WHAT ARE CHILDREN LEARNING?

Children are practicing identifying colors. They are making and responding to requests. Many children have difficulty with pronouns, and this is a good way to emphasize *he* for a boy and *she* for a girl. When they start playing on their own, the children are using fine-motor skills to refill the eggs with treats for their friends.

ADAPTATION AND ENHANCEMENT IDEAS

- You can add a size to your rhyme if you have big and little eggs.
- A customer can request a specific number of eggs.

ACTIVITY 161

Mouse House Color Game

MATERIALS

○ Markers
○ Paper
○ Velcro
○ Flannel board

GAME SETUP

Mouse House is a group game that can be played by the whole class or a smaller group. Find or create a pattern for a house. Draw several houses about five inches tall. Each house should be a different color. Put Velcro on the back of the houses and place them all on a flannel board. Without children watching, hide the mouse picture behind one house. Teach children the following rhyme:

"[*Color*] house, [*color*] house, [*name*] picked the [*color*] house.

Creep up softly to the door, quiet as a little mouse."

HOW TO PLAY

One by one, the children choose a color for their turn. Everyone sings the rhyme as the children approach their correct house and ring the doorbell. When they pull the house down, everyone should shout, "Gotcha!" The children clap and cheer when someone finds the hiding mouse.

WHAT ARE CHILDREN LEARNING?

Children are practicing color recognition. They are learning a new rhyme. Be sure to point out that *house* and *mouse* sound the same—they rhyme.

ADAPTATION AND ENHANCEMENT IDEAS

- Add a character behind the houses to match your theme.

- Houses could feature different characteristics that you are working on. For example, they can feature different shapes of doors or have different numbers of windows to present new challenges.

- Put pictures of the children behind all the houses, and ask children to find one of their friends when they ring the bell. The friend who is found gets to take the next turn.

Gobble, Gobble!

MATERIALS

○ A box large enough for a child to sit in

○ Pictures of different animals

GAME SETUP

This listening game can be played by small groups or by the whole class. Cut the lid off the box so one side is open. Show the animal pictures to the children and have them practice the animal sounds. Then teach a rhyme to the children that goes like this:

"Turkey, turkey, in the hay,

Will you come out if we sound this way?"

HOW TO PLAY

Ask one child to sit in the box and pretend to be a turkey in the hay. Show the rest of the children a picture of an animal and tell them to make the sound of that animal to complete the rhyme. The child in the box should listen to the sounds and pop out of the box if the other children say, "Gobble, gobble." Then ask another child to take the role of the turkey in the hay.

WHAT ARE CHILDREN LEARNING?

Children must listen carefully to the sounds their classmates are making, waiting for the correct sound so they can pop up from the box. They are practicing identifying animals and the sounds they make.

ADAPTATION AND ENHANCEMENT IDEAS

● Children can listen for other environmental sounds to match lessons your class is working on.

● Change the rhyme and use other animals and the sounds they make.

ACTIVITY 163

Moo, Roar, Quack

MATERIALS

○ Stuffed animals

○ Large bag

○ A CD or MP3 player and music

GAME SETUP

In this lesson, children will match animals to their sounds and practice different animal walks. To prepare, just fill the bag with an assortment of stuffed animals.

HOW TO PLAY

Ask one child to pull a stuffed animal from the bag and identify it. The child can share the sounds the animal makes and then demonstrate how the animal moves and sounds for the class. Then turn on some music, and encourage all of the children to move like their friend. When the music stops, the player gives the animal to another classmate. That friend brings the animal back to the front of the room and pulls out a new animal to discover.

WHAT ARE CHILDREN LEARNING?

Children are learning animal names and sounds. They are using their gross-motor skills to move like different animals. They are learning how to be a leader when it is their turn to demonstrate. They are learning to listen for the music and to know when to stop and start their animal walks.

ADAPTATION AND ENHANCEMENT IDEAS

● Add feeling cards to the activity. Children can pull an animal from the bag and then draw a feeling card. How does the monkey move if he is tired? How does a tiger sound if he is angry?

● Each child can pull out an animal at the end of the activity and listen for how the classroom sounds when everyone speaks like different animals.

ACTIVITY 164

Leap Frog Lily Colors

MATERIALS

○ Construction paper or felt
○ Markers
○ Pictures
○ Dice

GAME SETUP

Leap Frog Lily Colors focuses on movement, counting, and color recognition. Make several lily pads from different colors of felt or construction paper. On the back of each pad, place a picture or write a word describing a gross-motor skill—for example, *hop*, *crawl*, or *jump*. Position the lily pads in a circle in an open space on the floor.

HOW TO PLAY

Children shake the dice and then hop the specified number of spaces while they pretend to be frogs jumping on lily pads. They identify the color of their pad and then flip it over to see what gross-motor movement they must attempt. Everyone playing the game can try the balancing, hopping, or crawling movement too. The game is over when all the lily pads have been turned over.

WHAT ARE CHILDREN LEARNING?

Children are practicing gross-motor movements. They are also counting.

ADAPTATION AND ENHANCEMENT IDEAS

● New vocabulary words with corresponding pictures can be written on the lily pads. Pictures of emotions can be featured, and children can act out the emotions they land on or mention something that makes them feel that way.

● Make apples, and ask children to jump from apple to apple. Then place the apples on a tree after the gross-motor movement is completed.

ACTIVITY 165

Hugging Hearts

MATERIALS

○ Paper hearts

○ A CD or MP3 player and music

GAME SETUP

This is a game similar to Musical Chairs. Cut out different-sized paper hearts. Make sure one of the hearts is much bigger (about 3 × 3 feet) than the others. Spread the hearts on the floor in a large open space.

HOW TO PLAY

Turn on the music and encourage the children to dance and move around the room. When the music is over, the children all rush to a heart and stand on it. Every time the music is turned back on again, take away a heart. Instead of asking children to sit out if they don't have a heart, tell them to share hearts with their friends and stand on the big heart. By the end of the game, all of the children will be standing on one heart and holding one another. Make sure you join that hug. Everybody wins!

WHAT ARE CHILDREN LEARNING?

Children are learning to cooperate. They are helping one another and seeing that games do not need only one winner.

ADAPTATION AND ENHANCEMENT IDEAS

Use other shapes to match your theme. It is nice to focus on things that are best when shared: presents, foods, smiles.

ACTIVITY 166

Shake the Beanbag

MATERIALS

○ Beanbags

GAME SETUP

Beanbag play is a great way to work on gross-motor skills and balance. Beanbags are available in different sizes, colors, and shapes, including beanbag animals. This lesson presents some beanbag ideas to use throughout the day.

HOW TO PLAY

- Have children work in teams or with partners to toss beanbags back and forth.

- Have the group sit in a large circle and pass the bag around to music.

- Use beanbags to work on body parts. You can direct children to balance a bag on an elbow, knee, ear, or head.

- Introduce positional concepts using beanbags. (For example, you can ask students to place a beanbag behind a chair, under a foot, or below their chins.)

- Children can work on tossing beanbags into a basket or bucket.

- Beanbags can be used for children who find it difficult to sit during group activities. Sometimes holding and feeling the bag relaxes them and helps them focus on the lesson.

- Place beanbags on children's backs and ask them to crawl across the floor.

- Encourage children to put beanbags between their knees and try to hop or walk.

- Make a large game board on the floor, and ask children to try to hit targets. They can aim at the color or shape of their own beanbag. They can try to hit pictures of targets that match items in your story or theme.

- Place a target on the wall and tell children to try to hit it with their beanbags.

- Direct students to slide their beanbags on a smooth floor. Ask children to slide the beanbags between cones or to knock over pins, as in a bowling game.

- Encourage children to take off their shoes and walk on beanbags to see how they feel under their feet.

- Hide beanbags around the room, and ask children to go on a beanbag hunt. Build language when you talk about where the children found a hidden beanbag.

- See how many beanbags children can stack on their heads. See if they can walk on a balance beam with them.

ACTIVITY 167

Roll with the Wind

MATERIALS

- Straws
- Cotton balls
- Flat surface

GAME SETUP

This movement game builds up a child's core and shoulder strength. Give each child a cotton ball and a straw.

HOW TO PLAY

Tell the children to lie on their tummies and blow cotton balls with the straws. They will need a smooth, flat surface so the cotton can move easily. Provide a finishing point—for example, a pair of cones or cups—that children can use as a goal to blow their cotton to.

WHAT ARE CHILDREN LEARNING?

Children are building their lung capacity and using their core and shoulder strength to keep their upper bodies off the ground while they crawl along behind their cotton balls. They are using a self-devised strategy to keep the balls going in the right direction.

ADAPTATION AND ENHANCEMENT IDEAS

- Ask children to work in relay teams. When one child finishes blowing the ball, he can run back to the team so the next child can take a turn. Be sure each child has a personal straw to use.

- Try using a Ping-Pong ball instead of cotton. It will move much more easily and quickly along the floor.

- Encourage children to do experiments with other items, such as blocks or heavier balls. Discuss which ones move most easily and why they go faster.

- Two children can race, one with a cotton ball and one with a Ping-Pong ball. Keep track on a graph or chart of which ball wins. See if there is a pattern.

- Children can try blowing on things with rough, smooth, and sticky textures. Create a chart to see if the items go faster if the children blow through the straw or blow with their mouths. You can also provide them with party blowers to hit the objects.

ACTIVITY 168

Wrap It Again and Again and Again

MATERIALS

○ Boxes of different sizes

○ Wrapping paper

○ Ribbon

○ Treats or stickers

○ Music

○ CD or MP3 player

GAME SETUP

This present-passing game is particularly fun to play around the winter holidays. Place enough stickers or treats inside a small box so all of the children can take one. Wrap the package and tie ribbon onto it. Don't make the ribbon too tight; you want children to be able to work independently to undo it. Place this box inside another box and wrap it. Keep doing this until you have a very large wrapped package.

HOW TO PLAY

Ask the children to sit in a circle, and tell them that someone left this present for them. Play some music, and tell the children to pass the package around the circle. When the music stops, whoever is holding the package can begin to unwrap it. Start the music again, and continue passing the package around the circle. Keep passing and opening until the final box is revealed. The child who opens the last box can pass out the treats or stickers to the group.

WHAT ARE CHILDREN LEARNING?

Children are practicing gross- and fine-motor skills when they pass the package and open the wrapping paper and ribbons. They are excited to see what will happen next. Concepts like *open*, *smaller*, and *empty* can be discussed as the children continue to find new packages. They must listen and hear when the music has stopped and when it starts again.

ADAPTATION AND ENHANCEMENT IDEAS

Instead of sitting in a circle, the children can move around to the rhythm of the music. One child can hold the package. When the music stops, that child gives the package to another. The giver can share something nice about the receiver while that person opens the package. Then the music starts again.

ACTIVITY 169

Feed the Squirrel

MATERIALS

○ Tongs

○ Peanuts with shells

○ Four paper cups

○ Construction paper

○ Markers

GAME SETUP

NOTE: *Be aware of any peanut allergies among the children before playing this game.*

In this activity, children use tongs to feed an animal. Draw a paper squirrel or chipmunk (or use a stuffed animal) and place it at one end of the classroom. Paint each cup a different color: red, green, blue, and yellow. Place these next to the animal. Add colored marks on the peanuts, using markers in the same four colors. Make animal footprints and place them on the floor leading from the animal to the peanuts, which should be scattered on the floor in a different area.

HOW TO PLAY

The first player takes the tongs and follows the footprints to the peanuts. At the end of the path, the player uses the tongs to pick up a colored peanut and follows the path back to the animal. The peanut is placed in the correct colored cup for the animal to eat.

WHAT ARE CHILDREN LEARNING?

Children are practicing fine-motor skills when they use the tongs to pick up peanuts, hold on to them all the way back to the start, and place them in a cup. They are using matching skills when they look at the color on the peanut and match it to the correct cup.

ADAPTATION AND ENHANCEMENT IDEAS

- When all the peanuts are in the cup, children might take the peanuts out of the shells and eat them for a snack.

- Children can use tongs to pick up other items: White pom-poms can be used to fill up a bucket with snowballs. Crumpled papers can be thrown into a plastic bag for a spring cleanup or recycling theme.

ACTIVITY 170

Playground Tumble

MATERIALS

None required.

GAME SETUP

Take the children out to the playground. Demonstrate a three- or four-step sequence on the playground equipment. For example, go up the stairs, through the tunnel, down the slide, and over the bridge.

HOW TO PLAY

After the children have watched you, see if they can follow the same sequence on their own. Be available to help them with different parts of the sequence if they need assistance or have never used that playground equipment before. Give them turns being the leader, with others following the pattern they make on the equipment.

WHAT ARE CHILDREN LEARNING?

Children are practicing gross-motor skills that they may not have tried before. This will give them a new outdoor experience and may help them become more confident when they explore new playground equipment. They are following a pattern and remembering what they have watched.

ADAPTATION AND ENHANCEMENT IDEAS

- Suggest some moves that require children to work together on the equipment. For example, they can hold hands so one goes forward and one goes backward over the bridge, or they can slide down the slide together like a train.

- Use a ball during part of the sequence. Children can roll the ball down the slide or carry it over the bridge.

- Talk to the children about concepts used on the playground. Introduce such terms as *fast*, *under*, *high*, *around*, or *on top*.

- Make sure there is enough time so the children can make their own choices on the playground after the demonstrations. The playground is a great place to work on balance and coordination as well as simply enjoying time outdoors.

ACTIVITY 171

Puppy Run

MATERIALS

○ Stuffed toy dog

GAME SETUP

This is a variation on the game Gray Duck or Duck, Duck, Goose. Ask the children to sit in a circle on the floor in an open area.

HOW TO PLAY

One child can carry the stuffed dog around the outside of the circle and touch each child on the head, greeting each one by name: "Hi, Sally!" When the child is ready for a friend to chase her, she drops the puppy in the other child's lap. The child with the puppy chases her around the circle, trying to catch her before she finds the empty spot and sits down. The child with the puppy now goes around the circle and picks a friend. Make sure that everyone gets a turn and that the children cheer for both the chaser and the chased.

WHAT ARE CHILDREN LEARNING?

Children are practicing greetings. They are learning how to take turns and cheer for classmates. They are using gross-motor skills to get off the floor, run, and then plop down.

ADAPTATION AND ENHANCEMENT IDEAS

- Instead of calling out names, children can say colors or words from different categories—such as vehicles, farm animals, or clothing—before they drop the animal.

- Use stuffed animals or objects that match your theme in the classroom.

ACTIVITY 172

Knockout

MATERIALS

○ Hats
○ Beanbags or balls
○ Balance beam
○ Chairs

GAME SETUP

Position the balance beam between two chairs. Place a variety of hats the length of the balance beam.

HOW TO PLAY

Have children take turns choosing a beanbag and throwing it to knock one of the hats off the balance beam. Children can return the hats to the balance beam when they are done so other children can have a turn. Encourage them to cheer for their friends when it is their turn. After a few rounds, children should restock the beam and retrieve the beanbags or balls on their own. This is a good game for small groups and independent play. Children can keep track of how many hats they knock off and work to increase their personal best.

WHAT ARE CHILDREN LEARNING?

Children are practicing throwing skills and aiming at a target. They are practicing visual tracking when they aim at a specific hat and try to knock it off the balance beam.

ADAPTATION AND ENHANCEMENT IDEAS

- Children can use different sizes of balls to knock off the hats and talk about whether hitting the hat is easier with a large or small ball. Or children can use balls of different weights and discuss whether the heavier balls are more difficult to throw.

- Children can use a ball and a beanbag and talk about which one works better to throw.

- Use other items on the balance beam to go along with your theme, or challenge children by using smaller items on the balance beam, such as small stuffed animals, blocks, or cars.

- Children who are more skilled at throwing can stand back farther so they need to throw harder to reach the beam.

- If you use different types of hats, ask the children when those might be worn. If some are specific to occupations, discuss that.

ACTIVITY 173

Spoon Races

MATERIALS

○ Spoons

○ Plastic eggs

○ Baskets

GAME SETUP

Separate the children into two teams. Line the teams up in the classroom or outdoors. Give each child a spoon. Place two baskets with eggs in front of each team. Place two empty baskets some distance away.

HOW TO PLAY

The children at the front of each line scoop a plastic egg from a basket. They walk across the room, trying to balance the egg on the spoon until they reach a basket and drop the egg in it. Then they hop back to the start and tag the next person in line. The race continues until all children on both teams have completed the challenge.

WHAT ARE CHILDREN LEARNING?

Children are cheering for each other and working as a team. They are practicing balance and coordination when they move with an egg down the path. They are using fine-motor skills to keep the egg on the spoon.

ADAPTATION AND ENHANCEMENT IDEAS

- If there are children who have difficulty balancing, they can use spoons and eggs with small pieces of Velcro on them so the eggs stick to the spoons.

- This balancing game can be played with Ping-Pong balls, tennis balls, or beads instead of eggs.

- Children can use wooden spoons to see if they are easier or more difficult to balance.

ACTIVITY 174

Freeze and Go

MATERIALS

○ Music

○ CD or MP3 player

○ Instruments with distinct sounds

GAME SETUP

Choose quiet music to play. Teach children the cues that tell them to take different actions. Tie each cue to a particular musical instrument. For example, children can freeze when you strike a xylophone and begin moving when you bang on rhythm sticks.

HOW TO PLAY

Start the music and tell children to move around the room to it. Remind them to listen for and follow your musical cues. Use different styles of music so they can move in a variety of ways. Piano music may prompt them to move as if they are floating, while music with a drum beat may prompt them to stomp their feet.

WHAT ARE CHILDREN LEARNING?

Children are using listening skills to discriminate among different sounds. They are following directions to freeze and start moving again. They are using self-expression and gross-motor skills when they dance around to the music and their skill in balancing in whatever position they must freeze in.

ADAPTATION AND ENHANCEMENT IDEAS

As children become confident about their listening skills, you can choose instruments that sound more alike. For example, use two sticks and a stick with a wood block so the children have to listen more carefully.

ACTIVITY 175

Hamper Toss

MATERIALS

○ Clothes hamper

○ Socks

○ Shirts

○ Clothesline

○ Clothespins

GAME SETUP

For this game, position one child next to the hamper and the others several feet in front of it. Place a pile of clothing items next to the hamper. Hang the clothesline in a safe area and place the clothespins there.

HOW TO PLAY

The child by the hamper tosses clothing to the other children. When one of them catches a sock or shirt, that child tries throwing it into the hamper. When all the items have landed in the hamper, the children can work together to get it over to the clothesline and use the clothespins to hang up the clothing.

WHAT ARE CHILDREN LEARNING?

Children are practicing catching and throwing. They are using fine-motor skills and strengthening their fingers to pinch clothespins and hang up clothing.

ADAPTATION AND ENHANCEMENT IDEAS

● Use two hampers, one for socks and one for shirts, so children can sort as they throw. The items can also be divided by colors or solids and stripes.

● Also include a washing area. Provide a washer (box) and empty detergent bottles for washing the clothes.

ACTIVITY 176

Blanket Roll

MATERIALS

○ Large blankets

GAME SETUP

This is an obstacle game in which everyone can participate. The children will be learning about positional and special concepts while they travel through the obstacles. Set up four stations, as described below, with blankets at each station.

HOW TO PLAY

At the first station, four children hold the corners of a blanket while the other children crawl under it. They lift the blanket high and low to see if their friends can walk under it or need to crawl on their bellies.

At the second station, children take turns lying on the edge of a blanket. They grab the side and roll themselves up like hot dogs. Their friends can come over and pat on toppings like mustard, cheese, and onions. (Some children may not want to roll themselves up in the blanket, so allow them an extra turn at putting on toppings.)

The third station includes several sizes of blankets. Ask children to guess how many friends can fit on or under a blanket. They should practice counting while they test their predictions. The sides of a large blanket can be sewn together to explore how many children can fit inside.

The fourth station requires two adults. Ask them to hold the corners of the blanket while a child lies in the middle. They pick up the corners so the child is above the floor and can be gently swung in the blanket. The rest of the children can sing "Rock-a-bye [child's name]." The adults let the blanket down softly at the end of the song so the child can roll out.

WHAT ARE CHILDREN LEARNING?

Children are learning spatial concepts such as *high*, *low*, *on*, and *under*. They are making predictions and experimenting with their ideas when they count how many friends fit on the blankets. They are learning about sizes when they figure out that the big blankets hold more children than the small ones. They are singing songs and working together to hold the corners of the blanket and add toppings on their hot dog friends.

ADAPTATION AND ENHANCEMENT IDEAS

● Use blankets made from different materials and talk about their textures.

● Hold story time on one of the big blankets.

● Ask children to practice folding the blankets at the end of the lesson. They will need to work together to get the larger blankets folded neatly.

CHAPTER 6

Family Involvement

Involving the children's families is critical to the success of a preschool. Many families are busy and can't always visit their children's classrooms. In the Involving Families in the Home Setting section of this chapter, you will find activities that can be sent home with children. The activities engage them and their families and offer them opportunities to learn about each other while the children practice preschool skills. Additional lessons in the Involving Families in the School Setting section take advantage of those times when families can visit the preschool. Many of the ideas will be exciting enough to lure even the most reluctant families to spend more time there. The purpose of all of the activities in this chapter is to create a relationship between home and school, building a bridge to help teachers and families work together effectively.

ACTIVITY 177

The Quilt

MATERIALS

○ Cloth quilt squares of any color (about 6 × 6 inch)

○ Box

○ Hole punch

○ Ribbon or yarn

○ Art supplies

○ Note to families

SETUP

The children will make a room quilt by putting together pieces that have been decorated at home. Quilt squares can be purchased at quilting stores, many fabric stores, and through mail order companies. (Or perhaps you can find a friend or coworker to sew a finished edge that will prevent fraying around the squares of material.) You can also make squares out of paper if you don't have access to fabric.

INTERACT

Send home the quilt square in a box with art supplies, including glue, fabric paints, and scissors. Other fun materials are sequins, feathers, beads, eyes, and foam shapes. Add instructions and a note about the project in the box for families. The note should ask family members to decorate the square with their child and send it back to school when it is finished and dry. Tell parents they should feel free to use additional materials when creating their square.

When each child's square is finished, punch the squares and tie them together with ribbon or yarn. Display your quilt project in the hallway for other classes to see. Be sure your quilt has been completed before family conferences.

WHAT ARE CHILDREN LEARNING?

Children are working with their families to create something with their imaginations. Some squares will come back with abstract lines and shapes, while others will contain complex scenes. Each square is a unique expression that the child will treasure.

ADAPTATION AND ENHANCEMENT IDEAS

● Take a digital photograph of the entire quilt, make prints, and send them home with the children to share with their families.

● A similar activity can be done with puzzle pieces. These can be purchased commercially, or you can make puzzle pieces from tagboard. Title a bulletin board "Getting Together in Preschool" and put all the decorated pieces on it.

ACTIVITY 178

Create a Story

MATERIALS

- ○ Copies of an incomplete story
- ○ Pictures of different animals for the children to color
- ○ Markers or crayons
- ○ Note to families

SETUP

In order to develop language skills and give children a start with creative writing, make up a story with missing pieces. Here is a story sample you can use:

My Animal Adventure
Written and Illustrated by: _____

One day my mom took me to the _____. We saw a(n) _____. He had _____ that were the color _____. I thought it was funny when he _____. He liked to eat _____ and drink _____. Mom said he was too _____ to bring home, so we said "Good-bye" until next time. Tomorrow I'm going to ask Dad to take me to the _____.

INTERACT

Send home the story for children to complete with their family. Encourage them to add illustrations to the story.

WHAT ARE CHILDREN LEARNING?

Children become excited to find they will become the illustrator and author of their own story. They see how stories describe characters, settings, and events as they work inside the framework of the story.

ADAPTATION AND ENHANCEMENT IDEAS

- Ask parents to validate their children's answers by writing them in the blanks, even when they don't make much sense. Remind them that this is the child's story.

- When all the stories are finished, read them to the class and post them in the hallway or in a class binder in the reading center.

- Sometimes families don't complete projects that are sent home. If the work does not come back, be sure to complete the activity with the child at school.

Picture Perfect

MATERIALS

○ Tagboard circles

○ Note to families

SETUP

Children will share photos from home with the class in this take-home assignment. Ask them to take home a piece of tagboard cut in the shape of a circle and to decorate it. You will want to display these when they are done, so make the circles as big as your space will allow. Send the board home along with a note for parents.

INTERACT

Ask families to look through family photos with their child and find some pictures that can be placed on the board. Encourage them to talk about the photos while they are looking through them to decide which ones to use. Parents can attach the photos to the board and write captions about them. Display the circles where you can be confident they will stay safe. When the children bring in their circles, save time in your day to talk to the children about the pictures and their families.

WHAT ARE CHILDREN LEARNING?

Children are sharing information from home. They are using their memory skills to talk about the people and places in the pictures. This project is like a book report for young children. They need to stand up in front of the class and share information. As their teacher, you can ask questions and build their confidence about talking in front of a group. Allow their peers to ask questions as well.

ADAPTATION AND ENHANCEMENT IDEAS

- Ask for photos of specific things, like a family trip or a favorite holiday.

- If some children do not bring back the photo circles, you can take some pictures of them at school with their favorite things. You might even want to go on home visits and snap some pictures while you are there.

ACTIVITY 180

Homework Hurrah

MATERIALS

- Paper
- Stickers or prizes
- Note to families

SETUP

Young children enjoy having work to do at home. This is especially true if they have older brothers and sisters. Find simple things to send home with children to do. Make sure the papers are marked with a sticker or stamp indicating that it is homework. At this age, homework one time per week is sufficient practice.

INTERACT

Homework can be individualized to the needs of each child. For example, a child may be working on a specific speech sound. A sheet can be sent home asking the child to hunt for different common items that use that sound. Homework can also be something the entire class does. This can range from writing their name three times to drawing their room to finding two red things to bring back to school. Make sure the instructions are clear for parents on each homework assignment.

Keep a designated box where completed homework should be placed. When children turn in their homework, make corrections and draw a smiley face or add a star to show that it was graded. A little treat or sticker helps children know they have done good work and encourages them to continue on that same path.

WHAT ARE CHILDREN LEARNING?

Children are keeping track of their papers and bringing them back to turn in. If children don't have good support at home, they can do their homework during free play time at school. You will have to decide if there will be consequences for homework not brought back or rewards for the work that does come in. Homework at this age should be viewed not as a mandatory activity for families but as an opportunity to spend time with their children.

ADAPTATION AND ENHANCEMENT IDEAS

Ask parents for feedback on homework. See if you can make their experiences better. Some families may need a scissors or box of crayons to go home with their child in order to finish the projects. Provide a checklist on the feedback sheet asking if families need any of the items at home.

Take-Home Art Box

MATERIALS

○ Small plastic boxes or pails

○ Art supplies

○ Note to families

SETUP

In this activity, children make unique creations using materials that they will take home. Put together a small box of art supplies. For example, you can include a small plastic bag with beads, buttons, feathers, wiggly eyes, and sequins. Add scissors, glue, fabric paints, and pieces of construction paper. Include a note about the art box with instructions to create a picture using the materials in the box. Explain to families that they can add items from home if they wish.

INTERACT

When the finished projects return to school, display them in the hallway or on a bulletin board. Make sure they are visible during family conferences so children can remind their family about what they made together. Ask for feedback from families about the project. A short note asking them such thought-provoking questions as "What did you learn about your child?" or "What did you and your child talk about while completing the project?" can help family members think critically about the activity and evaluate the time spent with their child.

WHAT ARE CHILDREN LEARNING?

Children are working together with their families and being creative. They are using fine-motor skills to work with the art supplies and tools.

ADAPTATION AND ENHANCEMENT IDEAS

● Use the art box concept to create other art activities. Send home a paper plate and ask families to create an animal face or a mask.

● Send home cutouts of puzzle pieces for families to decorate. When these items come back to school, fit all the pieces together to make a classroom puzzle.

● Cutouts of people can also be sent home. Ask families to make a picture of their child. Create an "All About Me" board in the classroom or hallway. Ask the children to guess which friend is on the board, and place a photo of the child beside each creation.

I've Got a Secret

MATERIALS

○ Decorated bucket

○ Note to families

○ Index card

SETUP

Children take turns carrying home a secret bucket, which you can decorate with stickers, plastic jewels, or contact paper. They follow your directions to find and put an item inside and then bring the bucket back to preschool.

INTERACT

Ask families to help their children find an item that fits inside the bucket to bring back to school. Include an index card, and ask family members to write three clues on it about the secret item. Offer them some ideas, such as "Tell us the color" or "What sound does it make?" or "What does it feel like?" When the children bring the items back, ask the child to share the clues. The children can guess what they think is inside each bucket. Let each child pull the item out of the bucket so everyone can share the surprise.

WHAT ARE CHILDREN LEARNING?

Children are using descriptive language and thinking about relative size when they are choosing an item to fit in the bucket. They are learning how to put information together to guess the identity of the items. They must think about all three clues and how they are related.

ADAPTATION AND ENHANCEMENT IDEAS

● Send the bucket home with instructions to find something matching a certain color or shape.

● If some children do not bring their buckets back, you can ask them to find items in the classroom to share with their friends.

● Take pictures of the children with their items and add these to the classroom blog or photo album.

Backpack Home

MATERIALS

○ Backpacks

○ Books

○ Washable stuffed toy

○ Disposable camera

○ Snack

○ Note to families

SETUP

Children will have an opportunity to take home a bedtime backpack filled with the fun items listed above. Use plastic backpacks or bags, if you can find them, because they are easy to wash and sanitize after each use. If you are feeling generous, you can find stuffed toys at a discount store and let the children keep them instead of using washable ones.

INTERACT

Ask children to take home the backpacks with a letter to their families. In the letter, explain that this is a bedtime backpack. Tell families to let their child enjoy the treat before bed and then to snuggle down with them to read some stories to the stuffed animal.

Ask family members to take two or three pictures with the camera. Print the pictures and put the photos in a classroom album. Give your e-mail address to families who might like to send you digital pictures from their home camera.

WHAT ARE CHILDREN LEARNING?

Children are engaging with their family members when they take pictures and read to their animals. They are making connections between home and school.

ADAPTATION AND ENHANCEMENT IDEAS

● If there are tapes or CDs that go along with the stories, you can add these to the backpacks.

● Visit a local dentist and see if you can get toothbrushes or toothpaste to add to the backpacks.

● Consider adding treats for siblings, because they will probably become involved with the bedtime backpack. Add a flashlight for reading in bed.

ACTIVITY 184

Color Day Bag

MATERIALS

- ○ Bags
- ○ Colored paper
- ○ Markers
- ○ Crayons
- ○ Note to families

SETUP

Many preschool children practice color recognition. Assign a color to each child. Place paper, a marker, and a crayon of that color into the bag, along with a note explaining what to do with them.

INTERACT

Children and their families decorate the bag at home and find one item that is the same color to bring back to school and share with their class. Encourage families to decorate the bag with materials of the same color from home if they want to.

WHAT ARE CHILDREN LEARNING?

Children are exploring their homes with their families. They are forming a good understanding of colors and using matching skills.

ADAPTATION AND ENHANCEMENT IDEAS

- Send home shape bags and ask children to work on finding items of different shapes to share.
- Send home number bags, and tell children to locate a specific number of items. When the bags come back, the class counts the items.
- Ask children to provide clues about the items in their bag. The rest of the children can try to make connections among the clues and guess what the bag contains.

Data Collection

MATERIALS

○ Bag of typical classroom materials

○ List of preschool skills

○ Note to families

SETUP

Information about children is collected daily. It is crucial to obtain data from families as well. Send home a form listing preschool skills. Accompany it with a small bag containing typical preschool materials, such as a puzzle, blocks, paper, scissors, crayons, and a book.

INTERACT

On the checklist, provide clear spots for families to mark down what they observe their child doing. This can take the form of "yes" and "no" boxes, or it can offer blank spaces for parents to write in. The form shouldn't overwhelm parents. Make sure it is brief, so you receive good information. You can send home a form and materials several times during the school year, or you can use this information as an initial evaluation while you are first getting to know a child. Think about other ways to include family feedback in your reports and data collection.

WHAT ARE CHILDREN LEARNING?

Children are learning the importance of school. They are seeing their families' desire to reinforce schoolwork when their families work with them at home. You are providing parents with clear tools and opportunities to interact with and discover their child's unique skills.

ADAPTATION AND ENHANCEMENT IDEAS

● Complete this activity before family conferences or other meetings with family members so you can add their information to your reports.

● Bring the materials in your bag along on a home visit. Show parents what you are doing so they can follow through the next time the bag comes home.

● Leave a place on your form for families to write down questions or add other skills they see. Some parents will provide you with more information if you give them space.

ACTIVITY 186

Reading Center

MATERIALS

○ Index cards

○ Note to families

SETUP

This is a take-home activity that also becomes a great gift idea. Send home a note card asking families to write down the title and author of the book they most enjoy reading to their child. Ask other teachers, your librarian, and your principal to fill out cards as well.

INTERACT

Ask the children to draw a picture or find a line drawing that goes with their family's book choices. Glue the drawing on a half sheet of paper. Add the book title, author's name, and child's name. When you have completed all the pages, make copies to send home, bound into booklets. You have now created a favorite stories coloring book for each child.

WHAT ARE CHILDREN LEARNING?

Children are learning about literature and authors. When they color the pages of the book, they will become interested in reading some of the story choices of their friends. Most important, they are spending time reading at home with their family members.

ADAPTATION AND ENHANCEMENT IDEAS

- Be sure to notice if some of the favorites show up in book orders so you can point them out to parents.

- During the time you devote to this activity, make a trip to the school or community library.

- Try to find all the books at the library and put them on the bookshelf in your classroom for family conferences or meetings so family members can look at the choices.

- Other lists that are fun for children to share include favorite nursery rhymes and fingerplays.

- Create an "All About Me" book that features things such as favorite food, animal, color, and character.

Friendship Chain

MATERIALS

○ Outlines of people

○ Papers to complete

○ Note to families

SETUP

In this activity, the children discuss the qualities of friendship with their families and send materials back to school to display. Give each child an outline of a person, along with a paper titled "A good friend is . . ." Send along a box of art supplies if you feel it's needed.

INTERACT

Provide instructions for each family to decorate the outline and write down what it means to be a good friend. When the outlines are returned, attach them together hand to hand, creating a long chain of decorated friends. Add the "A good friend is . . ." comments above each child's outline.

WHAT ARE CHILDREN LEARNING?

Children are learning about friendship and identifying the characteristics of good friends. They are working with their families to create something that will become a classroom project.

ADAPTATION AND ENHANCEMENT IDEAS

Take a photo of each child and place it above their contributions to the chain. Ask them to choose one friendship trait they possess, and label their picture with it.

Traveling Notebooks

MATERIALS

- ○ Small spiral notebooks
- ○ Basket or box
- ○ Note to families

SETUP

Children work on responsibility at home and school. Bringing a notebook back and forth helps them learn how to turn in work each day when they arrive at school. Include a spiral notebook on your supply list for each child at the beginning of the year. Encourage the children to decorate their books so they get the feeling that they are important. Write a note to families at the beginning of the year explaining what the notebook is for. They don't need to write in it every day, but they can use it to let you know if they did something special with their child, like visiting a relative or going to a movie. They can also let you know if there is something in the child's backpack that you should look for, like a book order or a show-and-tell item.

INTERACT

Each day when the children get to school, they are responsible for putting their notebooks in a designated basket or box before they find toys to play with. You can check the notebooks for any messages from home and then put the books in the children's cubbies. This ensures that when they pack their bags, they will always have something to take home. It also means that you know where they are if you must send a message home. You can use the books to let families know when their child had a great day or fell down on the playground and scraped a knee. The notebooks allow families and teachers to communicate daily.

WHAT ARE CHILDREN LEARNING?

Children are keeping their books in their backpacks and keeping track of when their backpacks contain information. They may be telling you right away if the notebook contains a note from a family member. Be sure to tell them when you write in the notebooks too, so they can alert the people at home. Responsibility is the key lesson of this activity.

ADAPTATION AND ENHANCEMENT IDEAS

- Hang up a picture sequence to remind children of the day's starting routines. The sequence can illustrate hanging up a coat, hanging up a backpack, putting notebook in the basket, finding a toy.
- Once in a while, give a sticker or small treat to all the children who remember to put their notebooks in the basket.

ACTIVITY 189

Invite Them In

MATERIALS

○ Letter to families

SETUP

Some families need little encouragement to visit the classroom. Others need an invitation, so give them one! Send out an invitation at the beginning of the school year welcoming families into the classroom.

INTERACT

Leave a space on the invitation where families can write down a date and time when they want to join you, what they want to do in your room, and any supplies they may need for their project. Provide a list of ideas for family activities:

- Play an instrument for the class.
- Tell the class about their occupation.
- Read stories to the children.
- Plan a cooking activity.
- Plant flowers.
- Bring in pictures and talk about a trip.
- Teach a dance.
- Teach the class how to play a sport or game.
- Plan an art project.
- Play a board game.

Another idea is to hold a "Family Day." Invite all families to come to the classroom on a specific day. When they first arrive, ask children to give them a tour of the classroom, showing them its different areas. Plan a snack for families to enjoy with their children. Then have children perform a couple of songs or fingerplays that everyone can join. Be sure to have many completed projects displayed for this special time.

WHAT ARE CHILDREN LEARNING?

Children are sharing their families with their teachers and their class. There is no better way to build relationships between home and school.

ADAPTATION AND ENHANCEMENT IDEAS

Reverse this activity by making a home visit and sharing one of your skills with the family.

Family Game Day

MATERIALS

○ Tickets of different colors

○ Favorite classroom games

○ Invitation to families

SETUP

Create a game day for families. Send a written or e-mail invitation. Encourage each family to bring a homemade or favorite board game.

INTERACT

Set up centers around the classroom, one for each participating family. Prepare tickets for each game area. Ask each family to decide how many children they want to entertain at their center. Each game can correspond to a ticket color to control the number of children attending each game center. Children pick a color and go to that area to play the game. When they are finished, they bring the ticket back and choose another game area to join. Make sure your game day is long enough so all children can have their turn at several games. You want the experience to be positive for the children and their guests.

WHAT ARE CHILDREN LEARNING?

Children are learning turn-taking skills. They are proud to share their families' favorite games with the class.

☼ ADAPTATION AND ENHANCEMENT IDEAS

● Make sure you offer some game choices to families who want to participate but don't have a game to share. They can play one of the games listed in chapter 5.

● Hold several game days if many families want to attend. If you don't have enough space, you may want only one or two families to come in at a time.

Giving Back

MATERIALS

○ Fleece material

○ Scissors

○ Invitation to families

SETUP

This activity gives something back to the community. Invite families to your room to make fleece blankets with the children. Ask each family to bring a specific amount of fleece, or see if a local craft store will donate some. Provide some samples for families who cannot purchase the fleece.

INTERACT

When family members come in, ask them to work with the children to cut one-inch slits around two pieces of fleece. Then they tie the two pieces together. Find an animal shelter or pet store to donate the finished blankets to. Sometimes shelters will send a blanket home with an animal who has been adopted.

WHAT ARE CHILDREN LEARNING?

Children are learning compassion for animals and giving back to the community. They are learning how to use their fingers to tie and scissors to cut the fabric.

ADAPTATION AND ENHANCEMENT IDEAS

• Take pictures of the blankets at the shelter or pet store to show children how their items are used.

• Encourage them to join other ventures that will help people or animals. Teaching children about caring for others can start at an early age.

Stuffed Animals Come to School

MATERIALS

○ Camera

○ Extra stuffed animals

○ Index card

○ Letter to families

SETUP

Send a letter home to families to send their child's favorite stuffed animal to school. Send along an index card, and ask families to write down the animal's name, where it came from, and any interesting stories about it. They may also wish to take a photo of the toy.

INTERACT

Encourage families to complete this activity with their children and to spend time talking about this favorite toy. In the classroom, give children an opportunity to talk about their animals and to share the information recorded on the cards. Put the cards and pictures into a photo album for the children to look at. Provide stuffed animals for children who do not bring one from home.

WHAT ARE CHILDREN LEARNING?

Children are learning how to share something from home by relaying information about their favorite toy.

ADAPTATION AND ENHANCEMENT IDEAS

● Take pictures of the animals to use for later activities. When the pictures are printed, attach them to the descriptive cards. See if the children can remember who brought each of the animals.

● If your program doesn't allow stuffed animals, you can ask children to bring in a favorite toy.

ACTIVITY 193

Generational Greetings

MATERIALS

○ Camera

○ Letter to families

SETUP

Send a letter inviting grandparents or other elderly family members (or significant figures, such as ministers, coaches, or neighbors) to spend the day in the classroom, share a favorite story, or play a game with the children. If possible, talk to the visitors and find out what type of activities they want to do with the children. See if they need any supplies or materials to complete their activity.

INTERACT

Take photos of the children with their visitors. Make books or games available if your guests do not bring anything with them. Some guests will come in with elaborate ideas, while others may simply observe the children and spend time with their own grandchild. Create a visitor's center in the classroom on the day of the visit. Include art supplies, paints, and paper. Encourage each visitor and child to spend time in the area making a special card or other artwork. Take pictures of them and their finished work. After the visit, help children write letters to their visitors remembering the fun day, and send the letters and the pictures.

WHAT ARE CHILDREN LEARNING?

Children are learning the value of having an extended family. They are usually excited to have family and other visitors come into the classroom and want their friends to meet them.

ADAPTATION AND ENHANCEMENT IDEAS

- Decide if you want to invite many people or if it better suits your classroom to have only one guest at a time.

- Work with the children on greetings and introductions. Help them practice how to introduce their visitors to you and other adults or friends.

- Hold a Sibling Day, when children can invite their brothers or sisters. Or hold a Favorite School Person Day, when children can invite another teacher, staff member, or even the principal to their classroom.

INVOLVING FAMILIES IN THE SCHOOL SETTING

ACTIVITY 194

Friendship Collage

MATERIALS

○ Bags

○ Bottles of glue

○ Large piece of tagboard

○ Letter to families

SETUP

Send home a bag and a letter explaining that you are making a friendship collage and need their help. Ask family members to send enough items from home so each child can glue one thing on the collage. Provide suggestions, such as pieces of material, buttons, or cotton balls.

INTERACT

When the items have been brought in, sit down with the class and ask them to share their items. They can walk around the room and pass out what they brought from home. They can shake their bags first. Talk about the sounds and ask the children to guess what is inside. Once the items have been distributed, ask the children to make the collage. They will glue the pieces on the tagboard wherever they want. Limit the number of children working at one time to three or four. They can put their pieces on in phases rather than all at once, so each child gets the experience of working with different amounts of empty space and deciding where to place the pieces.

WHAT ARE CHILDREN LEARNING?

Children are sharing and taking turns. They are learning how to use glue and making their fingers strong by squeezing the bottles.

ADAPTATION AND ENHANCEMENT IDEAS

Some children may not bring items from home. Be sure to have a collection of things they can choose from. Store these items in the office or another classroom, and ask the children to go with another staff member on an adventure to pick out their items so they feel special.

ACTIVITY 195

Pocket Full

MATERIALS

○ Colored paper

○ Markers

○ Art supplies

○ Stapler

○ Tape

SETUP

This activity helps children show the people they care about how important they are. Ask the children to decide on a person in their life to whom they want to give this special gift. It can be a parent, sibling, grandparent, school friend, or someone else. Encourage children to practice fine-motor skills by folding, stapling, or taping a piece of paper in the shape of a pocket. Give them art supplies to decorate the pocket if they wish. Cut small colored pieces of paper to fit into the pockets.

INTERACT

Each of the children chooses a piece of colored paper and tells you something great about the special person. Write their words on the papers. Let them decorate the paper if they want to before placing it in their pocket. Ask open-ended questions if the children need help with ideas. Encourage them to present the pockets in person if they can.

WHAT ARE CHILDREN LEARNING?

Children are learning how to appreciate others. They are engaging in social awareness by giving a gift to someone they care about.

ADAPTATION AND ENHANCEMENT IDEAS

● This is a fun activity for Grandparents Day, Mother's Day, Father's Day, or Thanksgiving.

● It is also a unique way to send a thank-you to people who have interacted with or contributed to their class.

ACTIVITY 196

Rhyme Time

MATERIALS

○ Video recorder
○ A computer or playback to show the video clips to the children
○ Copies of nursery rhymes
○ Pictures of nursery rhymes to color

SETUP

This activity offers a way to involve parents in your class even when they are not physically present. Place drawings of different nursery rhymes for coloring in the writing and drawing center. Provide a bin to place the pictures in after children have colored them. Place all the pictures together in a book.

INTERACT

When family members come to class for meetings or conferences, ask them if they are willing to be recorded reading a nursery rhyme. Let them choose a rhyme and read it while you capture it on video. Share the videos with the children.

WHAT ARE CHILDREN LEARNING?

Children are sharing their family members with their classmates through these videos. They are learning nursery rhymes and using language to recite the rhymes with the video.

ADAPTATION AND ENHANCEMENT IDEAS

● Technology-literate family members can read rhymes and send them to you by e-mail.
● Send home a tape or digital audio recorder to each family and ask them to audio-record their favorite rhymes.

Family Favorites

MATERIALS

○ Index cards
○ Paper
○ Art supplies
○ Note to families

SETUP

This activity encourages families to share information with each other. Write a note to families explaining what they are to do. Send home index cards several times during the first part of the school year. On each card, ask the family about something that is a favorite:

● Who is the author of your favorite children's book?

● What family movie do you enjoy watching together?

● What is your favorite game to play as a family?

● What is your favorite family meal?

INTERACT

When the cards are returned, begin compiling a Family Favorites newsletter. Ask each child to decorate a sheet of paper or create a picture on the computer. Write the child's family favorites on the paper. Put all the favorites together in a packet to send home over longer breaks. Encourage families to try some of the favorites of other families.

WHAT ARE CHILDREN LEARNING?

Children are sharing their family preferences and traditions with their friends. They may complete some of the activities at home. The packet can provide some new ideas for families and help them bond and share experiences.

ADAPTATION AND ENHANCEMENT IDEAS

Ask families to send in favorite recipes and compile a recipe book to share with everyone. The children can add illustrations and their own thumbs-up reviews of a dish.

ACTIVITY 198

Newsletter

MATERIALS

○ Copies of newsletter to send home

SETUP

Write a monthly newsletter to send home to families. Use a template from a word-processing program or on the Internet (search for "newsletter template") to make the newsletter attractive and easy to read.

INTERACT

Use the newsletter to share information on monthly themes, birthdays, school topics, and special events or notices. Add pages that focus on developmental areas and ideas for parents to work on at home to complement your curriculum. These will provide parents with a connection between home and school. Include information about areas in which children are struggling, so parents know what skills to work on at home. Let parents know what books the children will be reading so they can talk about the stories or find the books at the library to reinforce lessons at school.

WHAT ARE CHILDREN LEARNING?

Children are making connections with their families and benefiting from sharing what they are learning at school.

ADAPTATION AND ENHANCEMENT IDEAS

- Ask other people, such as the center director or other staff members, to add items to your newsletters.

- Provide a monthly theme focus: for example, motor skills, language development, and social activities. Write the newsletter with those skills in mind. Include copies of activities that can be completed at home and brought back to school.

- Invite parents to write a column for the newsletter each month on their favorite topic.

On a Positive Note

MATERIALS

○ Note cards

○ Reward certificates

SETUP

Families need to hear about issues and problems involving their children. It is also crucial to tell them about the wonderful things that happen. Find ways to encourage parents and involve them in your school activities.

INTERACT

Make a point of telling families when their child has had a great day or learned a new skill. Keep a collection of notepads, fun note cards, or reward certificates to send home when you notice something special. This can be a child learning all of her colors or a child who was exceptionally kind to his classmate. Keep a log of your special notes so you reach out to each family with good news every month.

WHAT ARE CHILDREN LEARNING?

Children will receive positive feedback from home when their families receive the notes. They will learn that there is an important connection between what they learn at school and their family values.

ADAPTATION AND ENHANCEMENT IDEAS

- Make a phone call or send an e-mail to a family when a child has a good day.

- Take a photograph of the child's accomplishment to send home with the note or attach it to an e-mail.

- Ask the center director to sign the positive note to support your classroom, the children, and the importance of family connections.

ACTIVITY 200

Conference Notes

MATERIALS

○ Photographs

○ Copies or samples of children's work

SETUP

Meeting with families is important. They want to know how their children are doing and what they are learning at school. Here are some things you can include in children's portfolios to share at family conferences.

- Copies of children's projects
- Samples of work, such as self-portraits or handwriting, completed at different times during the year, that show progress
- Photographs of students working at different centers
- Notes from interviews with children to find out their favorite stories, activities, toys, and challenges
- Videos of children snacking, dancing, or participating in gross-motor games
- Checklists of skills children have learned
- Checklists of typical development for different ages
- Ideas for activities families can do at home to enhance their children's skills
- A follow-up questionnaire asking family members what information they want at conferences so you can tailor meetings to their expectations

- Lists of needed supplies that families may be able to provide
- Information from other professionals in your building
- Information about school or center policies

WHAT ARE CHILDREN LEARNING?

When you invite the children to join you for part of the conference, you help them make the connection between school and home. They are usually thrilled to show family members around.

ADAPTATION AND ENHANCEMENT IDEAS

- Many of these ideas work well for home visits too.
- At each conference, try to find out more about the families and how to make their children's classroom part of their lives. Visiting with parents will help you build a strong relationship that will allow you to make progress and enhance the skills of the children in your classroom.